USE LibreOffice Impress

Thomas Ecclestone

ISBN: 978-1500851170
ISBN-13: 1500851175

DEDICATION

This book is dedicated to Jay Lake. A great man, who will be missed.

CONTENTS

1 INSTALLING LIBREOFFICE

Step One – Download

❶Go to http://www.LibreOffice.org/download/LibreOffice-fresh/ in your browser

❷Click on the version of LibreOffice that you want to download. The screenshots in this guide are taken from version 4.2.5 for windows.

DOWNLOAD VERSION 4.2.5

❸If using chrome, the following box will appear at the bottom of the screen while the download is taking place. An estimate of how long the download will take is also shown.

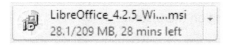

❹Once the download is finished, the following will appear at the bottom of the screen in chrome.

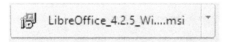

Other web browsers will vary.

Congratulations, you're ready to run the installer!

Step Two - Install

❶ Click on the LibreOffice install program. You can either find it at the bottom of your screen in chrome:

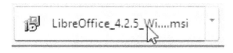

Or by opening File Explorer and selecting the download folder:

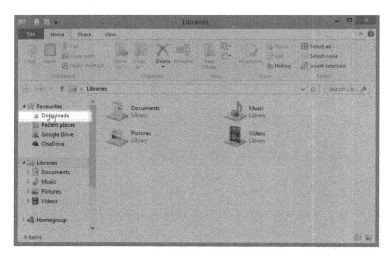

Then double clicking on the installer

2 The LibreOffice installation wizard will appear

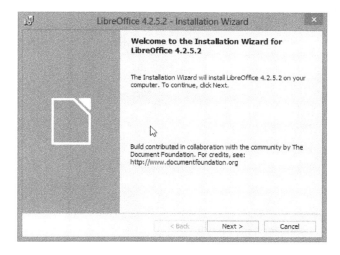

Click on

3 In the next dialogue you will be given the option of a typical or custom install. I recommend simply using the typical install.

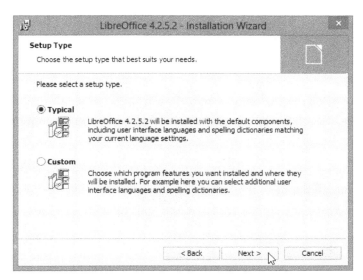

If you are happy with the typical install click

If you want to install a custom installation see "How to run a custom installation" below.

4 The next screen gives you a few more options. I recommend you click on install

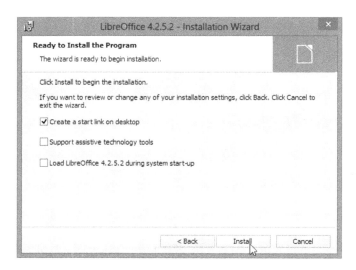

Selecting ☑ Support assistive technology tools will install tools that LibreOffice provides for people with various disabilities.

Selecting ☑ Load LibreOffice 4.2.5.2 during system start-up will mean that LibreOffice will start when the operating system starts. It's useful if you use LibreOffice almost all the time but may slow down loading the operating system.

When you are happy with your options click [Install]. If you are not happy with any choice you've made you can go back to an earlier choice by clicking [< Back].

5 A user account dialogue will appear. Click "Yes", "Allow" or "Ok".

6 A progress dialogue will appear:

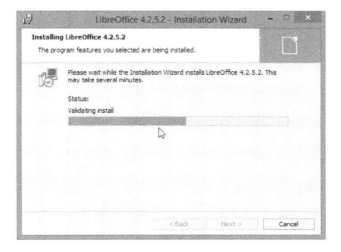

Wait until it is finished

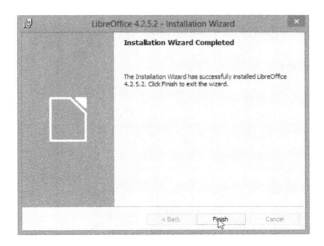

and click on
```
Finish
```
.

How to run a custom installation

Run the install procedure above, but in step instead of selecting

 Typical

LibreOffice 4.2.5.2 will be installed with the default components, including user interface languages and spelling dictionaries matching your current language settings.

select

 Custom

Choose which program features you want installed and where they will be installed. For example here you can select additional user interface languages and spelling dictionaries.

Then click on

❷To find out if there is available space for the feature set you've

selected click on

The following dialogue will appear:

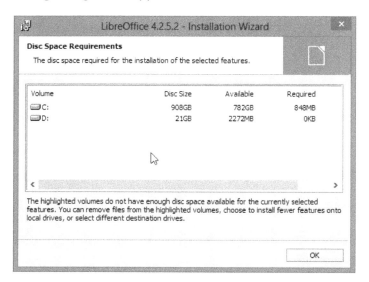

Notice that the column Available shows how much space your disk contains, and Required shows how much disk space your installation has available.

In the above example, we're good to go.

Click 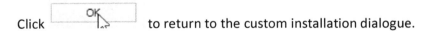 to return to the custom installation dialogue.

❸ To change the location the program will install to select change

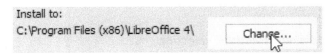

A location selection dialogue will appear:

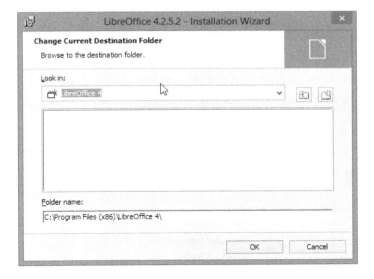

Clicking on the ⌄ next to the look in location will provide you with a list of folders

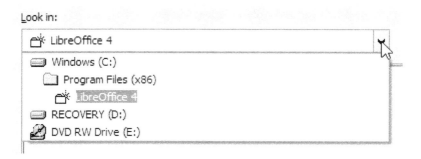

which you can select from, going up or down as necessary.

You can add a new folder by selecting

Or you can simply type the file location in the box provided

I don't recommend changing the file location UNLESS your default drive doesn't have enough room for the installation to work.

❸ To install a new language

Click on the next to

A list of languages will appear:

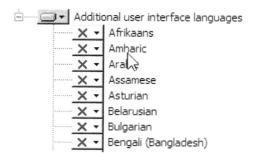

Scroll down to the language you want, and click on the

Select `This feature will be installed on local hard drive.` if you want it installed on the local hard drive or `This feature, and all sub-features, will be installed on local hard drive.` if you want sub features such as spell check and custom fonts to be installed. I recommend this option.

❹ To install non-English language dictionaries:

Click on the ⊞ next to ⊞ ▭▾ `Optional Components`

Click on the ⊞ next to ⊞ ▭▾ `Dictionaries`

Scroll down to the dictionary you want, and click on the `✕ ▾` by its name, for example:

`✕ ▾` `Bengali`

Select
`This feature, and all sub-features, will be installed on local hard drive.`

❺ Other Optional Components

LibreOffice installs most components by default. The only exception is ActiveX components. If you don't need a particular component and you are low on space you can click the ▭▾ by its name and select `✕ This feature will not be available.` but I do not recommend doing this. It will limit the facilities your LibreOffice installation can provide to you.

Some people may need ActiveX controls, in which case you can select the `✕ ▾` by `✕ ▾` ActiveX Control and `This feature, and all sub-features, will be installed on local hard drive.` . I don't recommend doing this unless you know that you will need ActiveX controls since it can slow down LibreOffice and it's an unusual requirement

❻ Once happy with the options you have selected click on . A File type dialogue will appear

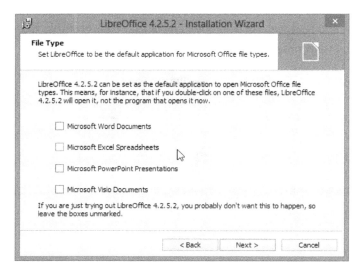

I recommend leaving the defaults on this, but simply check the box next to the file types you want to associate LibreOffice with and click 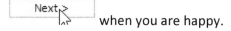 when you are happy.

❼ You are now on the installation dialogue that is the last step in "Install LibreOffice" above.

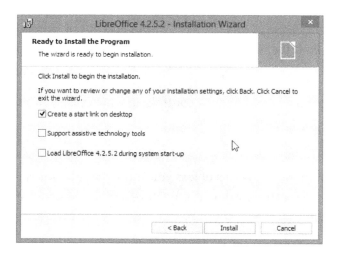

Selecting ☑ Support assistive technology tools will install tools that
LibreOffice provides for people with various disabilities.

Selecting ☑ Load LibreOffice 4.2.5.2 during system start-up will mean that
LibreOffice will start when the operating system starts. It's useful if you
use LibreOffice almost all the time but may slow down loading the
operating system.

When you are happy with your options click Install . If you are
not happy with any choice you've made you can go back to an earlier
choice by clicking < Back .

❽ A user account control dialogue may appear. Click "Ok", "Yes" or
"Allow" depending on what version of windows you use.

❾ A progress dialogue will appear.

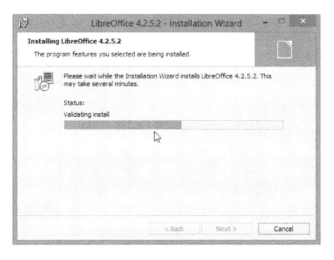

Wait until the installer finishes:

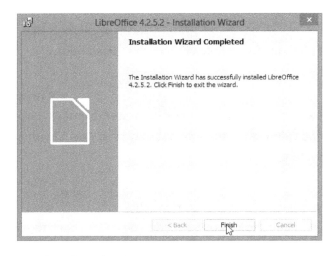

And click on  .

To Run

To run LibreOffice Impress double click on its icon on the desktop

 or select its tile in the start screen  or search for it

Create a New Document

If you've started the main LibreOffice program you will see the following window:

12

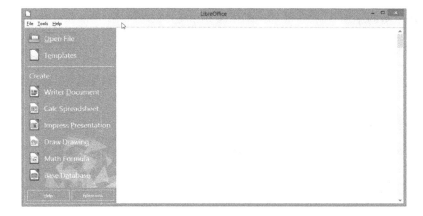

To create a new presentation click on:

To open an existing document

In the main LibreOffice window, click on

Select the file you want to open:

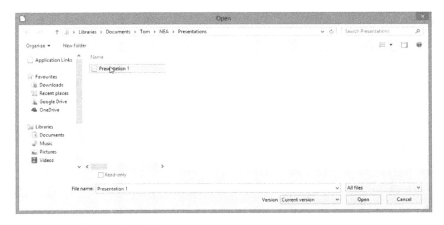

And click .

Either way you'll see the LibreOffice Impress screen for the first time:

Next Chapter

In this chapter I've shown you how to install LibreOffice, and how to start a new presentation.

The next chapter will be a short tutorial explaining how to create a simple slideshow. It'll explain the main features of the program while showing how to actually use it.

It'll be fun!

2 FIRST STEPS

The opening window

When you first open Impress it can have quite an intimidating feel.
There are a lot of things in the main window. The centre of the main
window (5) is the most important part of the program showing you the
slide that you're editing at the moment.

Slides and Slideshows

A presentation is made out of slides and a slideshow. You can think of a slide as a single page of the presentation, an acetate on an overhead projector, or a 35mm slide.

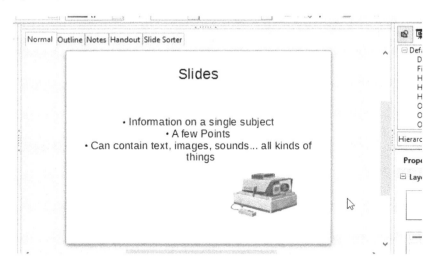

A slideshow is an ordered list of slides that you can display on an overhead projector of computer screen

1 : Menu Bar

File   Edit   View   Insert   Format   Tools   Slide Show   Window   Help

The menu bar gives you options like File, View, help which allow you to control what the program does.

2: Task Bar

The task bar has icons that allow you to print, create new documents and many other features that will come in handy later on. Notice that when you're working in different views or doing specific tasks there may be extra icons on the task bar related to what you're doing at the time.

3: Slides

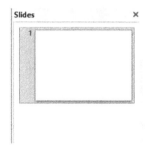

You can use the slide Dockable window to navigate between slides in the slideshow, or add, delete and move slides.

4: View Tabs

You can move between different modes which are used for different things, such as Normal (to make a slide) Outline (Shows a list of different topic titles in the slideshow) and so on.

5: Main Viewable Window

This is the window where you can see the current view. For example, in normal view (above) you can create or edit a slide.

6: Styles

We'll discuss styles later on in the book, but a short explanation is that a style is used to give your presentation consistency in design and appearance so all text is the same throughout the document, and the size and format of the presentation is the same.

7:Properties

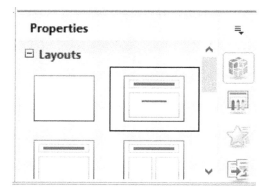

The Properties Dockable window allows you to control the layout and many other features of the slide and slideshow.

8: Draw Taskbar

Allows you to draw basic shapes and insert images into the slide.

9: Information

Gives you information about the current slide such as where the mouse is, what area has been selected, and the current slide position in the slideshow.

10: Zoom

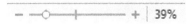

Magnify or shrink the area displayed in the viewable window (5). In other words make the slide appear larger or smaller. If you make it too large you might have to scroll across it to edit the part of the window that you want to change.

Don't worry!

Although there appears to be a lot going on in the Impress main window the reality is that you'll pick it up very quickly. The easiest way to pick it up is to start using it right away. I'm going to make the simplest presentation ever...

Presentation On LibreOffice Impress

For the rest of this chapter we're going to create a new slideshow using LibreOffice Impress. While it won't be the most impressive slideshow in the world it'll be a beginning. We're going to:

1. Create a new Presentation
2. Edit a slide title
3. Insert a bullet list

4. Insert two new slides
5. Delete a slide using the Slide Dockable window
6. Run a slideshow
7. Save a presentation

While the slide will be pretty basic this is all you need in order to create slideshows in LibreOffice Impress.

Step 1: Create a new Presentation

Within LibreOffice main window

When you click on the icon you open up the LibreOffice main window.

Click on Impress Presentation in the sidebar on the left to create a new Impress Presentation.

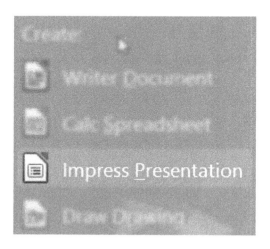

Within LibreOffice Impress

If you are already in LibreOffice Impress all you need to do to create a blank presentation is press ctrl+n (in other words hold the control key down and press N).

Step 2: Edit a slide title

In the main viewable area you should see a blank slide. Click at the top where it says "Click to add title":

Click to add Title

The rectangle surrounding the text is highlighted in blue and you can add text to the title box:

Impress Example

Once you're finished you can click off the title by clicking on the grey area around the slide OR by clicking on the next object to edit on the slide.

Step 3: Insert a bullet list

In the main viewable area click on the larger rectangle where it says "Click to add text":

You'll see the box highlighted, ready to enter some text:

In the task bar click on the bullet list icon you'll notice that when you click it you see a bullet appear in the text box:

Type in a few lines of text. Press enter between each line.

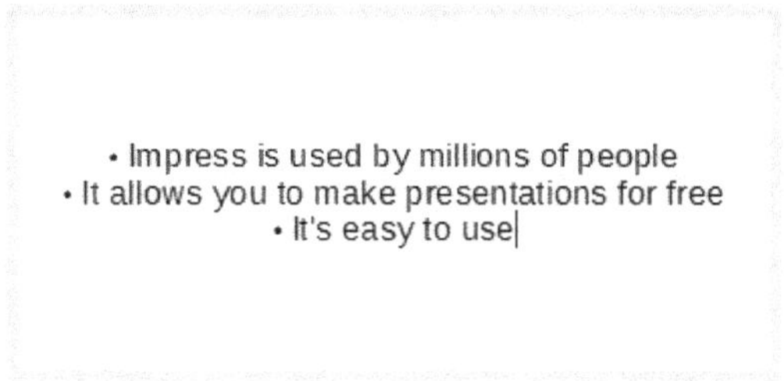

• Impress is used by millions of people
• It allows you to make presentations for free
• It's easy to use|

When you're done, click on the grey area around the slide. You've already done something pretty special... made your first slide in LibreOffice Impress. It looks like:

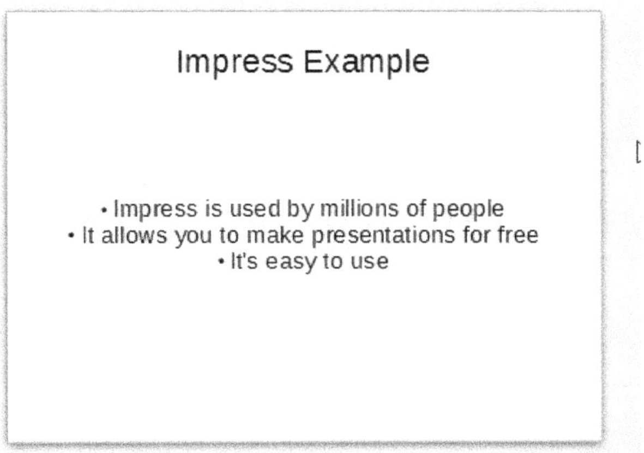

Impress Example

• Impress is used by millions of people
• It allows you to make presentations for free
• It's easy to use

While the rectangle around the title and the text box has disappeared because you've put text in those objects you can click onto either and begin editing again.

Step 4: Insert two new slides

LibreOffice wouldn't produce very good slides if you could only make a single slide. Most presentations have more than one slide, some long presentations may have thirty or forty!

It's pretty easy to add a slide in LibreOffice Impress. You can use the Slide Dockable Window to do it (which is to the left of the slide we're editing).

You'll need to right click on the slide immediately before the slide that you want to insert:

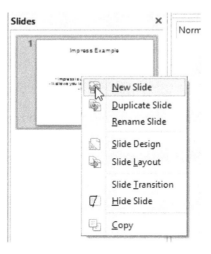

Since at the moment we've only got one slide, that's easy - you want to insert after slide 1! Right click on slide one and click on New Slide. You'll see the new slide appear in the main viewable area and on the slide Dockable window.

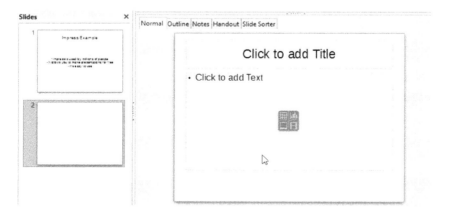

Edit the title again (see above) to read "Slide 2". Note that when you've finished the slide changes in the Slides Dockable window

Also note that on the slides Dockable window besides each slide is a number - the current position in the slideshow. Slide 1 is "Impress Example".

Right click on slide 1 and click on New Slide. Note that the new slide is inserted between Slide 1 and Slide 2:

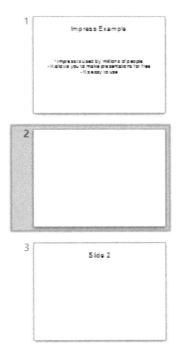

So the former slide 2 becomes slide 3.

Step 5: Delete a slide using the Slide Dockable window

If you want to delete a slide simply right click on it in the slide Dockable window and click on Delete Slide. In this example I'm deleting slide 2 (the blank slide we just inserted):

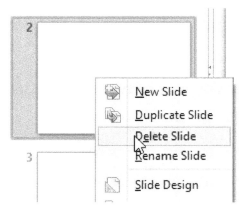

When you delete a slide you remove it from the slideshow altogether and all subsequent slides are renumbered in the slide Dockable window:

Step 6: Run a slideshow

Press F5 to start the slideshow and the left mouse button to advance to the next slide. When you've finished the presentation you'll see a black screen with click to exit presentation at the left top hand corner. Click the left mouse button again to close the presentation.

Note that at this point we've done a presentation on impress. You'll often have to set up a projector to get the most out a presentation but that's quite a simple matter.

Step 7: Save a presentation

In the File menu click save as ![Save As Ctrl+Shift+S] . A save as dialogue will open. This works in the same way as any other Save as Dialogue.

Make sure you are in the right directory (your directory will vary compared to mine)

↑ 🔊 ▸ Libraries ▸ Documents ▸ Tom ▸ NEA ▸ Presentations   ∨ ↻

Change the file name field to something appropriate

File name: Untitled 1   ∨

maybe, in this case, Impress Example

File name: | Impress Example|

And click ☐ Save .

Next Chapter

In this chapter I've described the main features of the LibreOffice Impress program and shown you how to insert, delete, and edit slides. I've also shown you how to create and save presentations.

The next chapter will show how to improve the looks of a presentation.

3 BASIC SLIDE DESIGN

In this chapter I'm going to show you how to make good looking slides, including:

- Choosing different slide designs
- How to move objects
- How to format text
- How to insert images
- How to insert automatic fields like name, date and page number
- How to change background and foreground colours
- How to make a presentation greyscale or black and white

This chapter really gets to the meat of how to make a slide that looks good without too much effort

Choosing different slide designs

On the bottom right hand side of the screen is a Dockable window that by default opens in the Properties view:

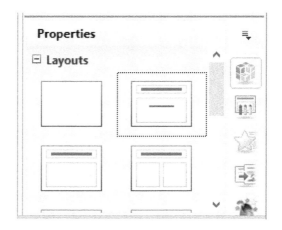

If the Dockable window isn't in the Properties view click on to make sure that it is in the correct view.

Under layouts there are pictures of a number of designs. You can scroll down to find the design you want. Once you've found the right design click on it. For example if you click on "Title, two content and content" from the scrolling area:

The slide you are working on will change to reflect the standard design you've just chosen:

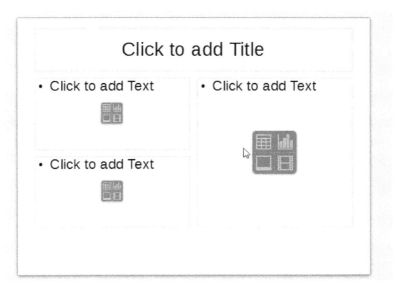

It's often best to decide on your slide design before you write any content. This is because sometimes you lose material when you decide to go from one slide design to another. In the above example if you went from a slide with three content boxes to one with only two, LibreOffice would have to lose the information stored in a content box.

One of the most interesting options is the Blank slide design:

Sometimes you might want to design a slide from scratch. The blank slide design choice will give you a slide that is empty which you can then insert different types of objects and design in any way you chose.

Inserting a text object

Chose the Blank Slide design in the Properties Dockable window (see above).

At the bottom of the screen is the draw toolbar:

Click on the Text Icon

T

Go to the point in the slide you want to insert the text and click with the left mouse button. Move the mouse to the far right where you went the text to end:

When you let go you'll see the outline for the text box:

You can type in whatever text you want:

This is some text
When you press enter you go on to a
new line

Click outside the blue line of the text box to deselect it. The blue outline will disappear.

This is some text
When you press enter you go on to a
new line

 If at some point you want to edit the text again you can simply click on it and the blue outline will reappear.

How to move objects

To move an object click on it. For example, click on the text box you just added. A blue outline will appear around it. Move your mouse over the blue outline until you see a cross pointer:

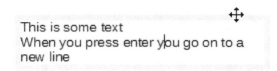

Click on the outline and you'll see some squares. These squares are for resizing the object or rotating it.

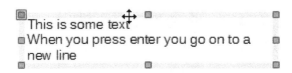

Click anywhere on the outline that isn't a square and hold the mouse button down. Move the mouse to wherever you want the text box to go. You'll see a faint ghost image appear. You're moving the object to wherever the ghost is located:

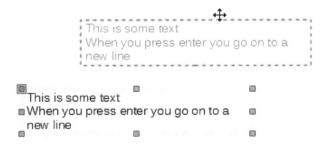

If you change your mind right click and you'll cancel the move. If you're happy with where you've moved the object let go of the mouse and the object will move to that location.

It's important that when you want to move text around the screen you move the object it's located in using the method above. People that are used to word processors often simply press enter to move text down. While this appears to work it often creates problems and errors as you change the design.

How to format text

Formatting text means changing its appearance. For example you can change the font, the font size, add emphasis or change the font colour.

When formatting text the first thing you need to do is to select it. Go to the bottom right hand corner of the text and you'll notice the mouse pointer changing to an capital I.

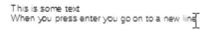

Click the left mouse button and hold it. Then move the mouse to the top left hand corner of the text you want to change. It'll be highlighted to give a visual clue of what text you've

selected

The Text taskbar

In the task bar you'll see the text taskbar. It contains a lot of options that are useful when you want to format text:

Changing the Font

Select the text you want to change (see above) and click on the arrow next to the Font Name combo box. This is the box at the far left of the text taskbar.

You'll see a list of Fonts. Click on the one you want from the box

The font of the selected text will change to your selection:

Changing the Font Size

Select the text that you want to change. To the right of the Font Name box is the Font Size box . Click on the arrow on the right:

You'll see a list of sizes. Chose the one that you want. Remember you can scroll up or down to find the right size:

Click on the font size you want. The text you've selected will get larger or smaller depending on the size you've chosen:

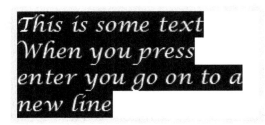

Because presentations are often displayed to large numbers of people I generally think that larger text is better than smaller text. Size 28 is often a good choice. This allows people to see the text at the back of the room.

Such large text means that you can't have too much information on any slide. This isn't a problem since you'll generally only want to include the main points of a presentation.

Changing the Font Colour

Select the text that you want to change. On the right of the Text taskbar is the font colour icon . Click on it and you'll see a list of the colours available.

Click on the colour you want:

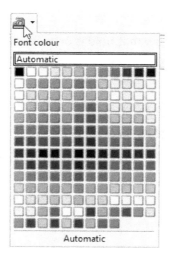

Your text will change to the chosen colour:

This is some text
When you press
. enter you go on to a
new line

You can click on Automatic to return it to the default colour:

When selecting colours make sure you consider whether your projector or computer screen can display colours. Almost all can these days, but if you're going to use a large range of technology it might be simplest to keep the colours greyscale or black and white.

Adding emphasis

To make your text bold first select the text you want to change. Then click on the bold icon in the text taskbar. the bold icon will change so it's highlighted to show that bold is on and the text you've selected will change to bold too:

This is some text
When you press
enter you go on to a
new line

If you click on without selecting any text, it'll turn off bold for any new text you add:

This is some text
When you press
enter you go on to a
new line without
bold

In the same way, if you turn bold on without selecting text you can add bold text in the middle of other text. You can also highlight a section of text and make it bold or not bold.

Adding Italics

Select the text you want to make italic and click on in the text

taskbar. The icon will change as above to show Italics is on .

This is some text
When you press
enter you go on to a
new line without
bold

You can click on  to turn it back off. You can also turn it on or off when no text is selected just like bold.

Adding Underlining

Use Underlining like bold and italics by clicking on  to turn it on

This is <u>some</u> text
When you press

And  to turn it off.

Changing the Alignment of Text

Alignment is the position of text in a text box. The alignment icons are in the text taskbar.

First, select the text you want to align.

Centre alignment

Centre alignment spaces out text so each line is in the middle of the textbox:

> *This is some text*
> *When you press*
> *enter you go on to a*
> *new line without*
> *bold*

Once you've selected the text click on the centre icon ⊞ to centre align it.

Right Alignment

Right alignment moves text so the left is jagged and the right is aligned to the edge of the text box:

> *This is some text*
> *When you press*
> *enter you go on to a*
> *new line without*
> *bold*

Once you've selected the text click on the Right Align icon ⊟ to Right align it.

Justified

Justified adds extra space so each line fills out the whole text box. Note that the first and last line isn't always perfectly justified. This depends to an extent on options you can select.

This is some text
When   you   press
enter you go on to a
new ⊥ line   without
bold

Once you've selected the text click on the Justified icon ⊞ to Justify it.

Left Alignment

This is the opposite of Right Align. The Left hand side is made straight while the right hand side is justified. This is probably the most usual setting for western languages:

This is some text
When you press
enter you go on to a
new line without
bold

Although most text objects left align by default you can select any text

you want to left align then click on the Left Align icon ⊞ to make the text aligned left.

How To change bullets and numbering

Highlight the text where you want to change the bullet and numbering format. Press the Bullet and Numbering icon 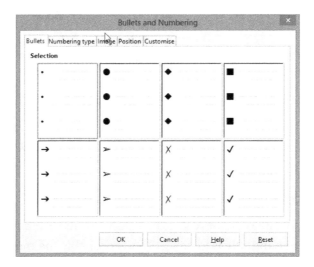 . You'll see the Bullet and Numbering dialogue

Chose the format that you want from the list of bullets by double clicking it, or click onto the numbering type tab for a numbered list.

How to change the case of text

Select the text where you want to change the case.

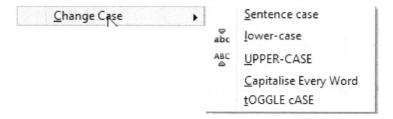

Click on the option that you want.

Sentence case to change the text to normal sentence structure (i.e. capitalised first words, lower case the rest). Lower-case makes all the words you've selected lower case. UPPER-CASE does the opposite. Capitalise Every Word makes every word a capital, and toggle case means that any letter that was lower case will be upper case and vice versa.

How to format a paragraph to indent text automatically

You can automatically indent text using the paragraph formatting options. First select the paragraph(s) you want to format:

This is a paragraph of text. You can control some of the features of it, like indentation.

Then click on the Format Paragraph icon in the text toolbar.

You'll see the Format paragraph dialogue. You want the **Indent** options.

If you want to indent the leading edge of the text, so each line is

indented on the left (see example)

Increase the Before text indentation

Before text: 0.00cm

You can indent the following edge (i.e. indent from the right margin) as in the below example

by using the After text indentation options.

After text: 0

Finally, you can use the classic English language indentation of an indent on the first line of a paragraph e.g.

by using the First Line indentation option:

First line: 1.80cm

Click OK when you're happy.

How to format a paragraph to control spacing.

You can automatically control the space between paragraphs using the paragraph formatting options. First select the paragraph(s) you want to format:

Then click on the Format Paragraph icon ¶ in the text toolbar.

You can add space above a paragraph or below a paragraph by setting the options. Where you have two paragraphs these figures are cumulative, so you'd add them both together. I normally suggest using only one of these options at a time since I think that's best.

Spacing

Above paragraph: 0.00cm

Below paragraph: 0.00cm

By default, LibreOffice Impress adds space between paragraphs of the same style but you can toggle this off by clicking on the

☐ Don't add space between paragraphs of the same style
square   .

You can also change the Line Spacing between lines of the same style using options in this dialogue.

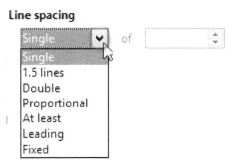

Click OK when you're happy with your choices.

Changing the background colour of text

By default the background of a text box is transparent. If you want to change the colour of the text box click into it, then

in the Format menu.

Click on the down arrow next to fill.

You can chose the Fill type that you want. Colour gives you a single colour, gradient gives a fade effect, hatching gives you a hatching effect, and Bitmap fills the text box with a background picture.

Fill

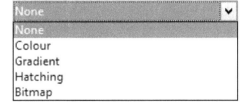

If you select anything apart from Bitmap you'll get a range of options to

chose from:

With a preview box below the options to show you what your choice will look like.

Bitmap does provide you with a list of options as above but it also provides you ways to control the offset, and many other features of how LibreOffice will display the bitmap. It's a bit beyond the scope of this book to explain how to use these features; I'd recommend using the help function if you want more details.

How to Cut Text

Select the text that you want to copy.

- Text **is in front of** box
- This is the second line

Press Ctrl+C to copy the text to the clipboard.

How to Copy Text

Select the text that you want to copy.

- Text **is in front of** box
- This is the second line

Press ctrl+X to cut the text. You'll see that the selected text disappears:

- Text f box I
- This is the second line

The selected text has been cut to the clipboard. You can recover it by pasting.

How to Paste Text

Go to the place in the document that you want to paste the text in the clipboard to.

- Text f box
- This is the second line ⌶

Press Ctrl+V to paste:

- Text f box
- This is the second lineis in front o|

How to Undo Changes

Everyone makes mistakes. But LibreOffice makes it easy to rectify them.

If you click on the undo button in the taskbar ↶ ▾ the last thing you did in LibreOffice Impress will be undone. LibreOffice allows multiple levels of undo, by clicking the down arrow next to the undo button you get a list of all the actions you've made:

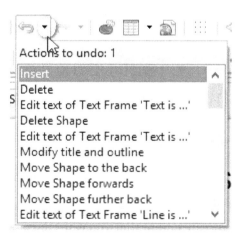

You can keep on going back to the last place in the document that you were happy.

How to Redo

If you made a mistake - undoing too many steps - you can change your mind too by pressing the Redo button to redo the last step, or the down arrow to redo multiple steps:

How to insert images

To insert an image hover your mouse over images in the insert menu then click on From File:

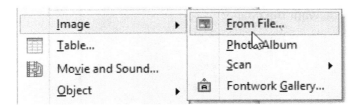

A file open dialogue box will be displayed. Change the directory and select the file like usual.

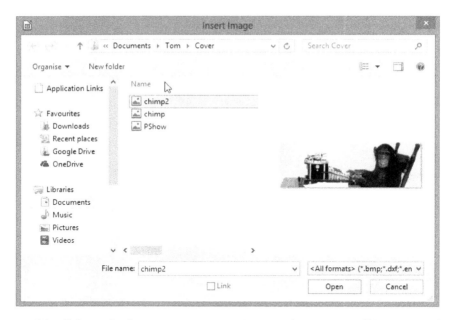

Double click on the image you want to insert. The image will be inserted into your slide.

To Move an Image

You can move an image in the same way you moved a text box. Click anywhere on the image and hold down. Then move the mouse to the location you want the image:

Let go when you're happy.

How to Resize an image.

Click on an image once. You'll see boxes appear on the edge of the image. The ones in the corner allow you to resize the image diagonally

Click on it and move the image so it's larger or smaller. You'll see a ghost image of what it'll look like. Let go when you're happy.

The rectangle in the middle of the border allows you to move that border alone. This "stretches" the image.

One thing to note is that when you increase the size of a picture you're not increasing the amount of information that LibreOffice has for that picture. LibreOffice can 'guess' the missing data but if you increase the size too much the image will become blurry and lose definition.

How to insert a date

If you want to insert the current date without it being updated or changed later, hover your mouse over fields in the insert menu and click on 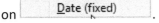 .

LibreOffice can also automatically update fields when you open the file or select the update option. These fields are called variable fields. You can insert a variable date field (one that will change when LibreOffice updates) by hovering your mouse over fields in the insert menu and clicking on  .

How to insert a Time

If you want to insert the current time without it being updated or changed later, hover your mouse over fields in the insert menu and click on . For a time field that will change when LibreOffice updates fields chose 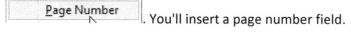 .

How to insert page number

Hover over the fields item in the insert menu and click on  . You'll insert a page number field.

You can move the page number in the same way as a image, by clicking on it and holding the button down then moving the mouse.

If you want to insert a page count field hover over fields in the insert menu then click on 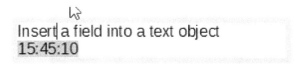.

Inserting a field in a Text Object

In this chapter I've already told you how to insert a text object. When you are editing the text in a text object you can insert a field such as Time or Date by hovering your mouse over the field item in the insert menu and selecting the field type you want to insert.

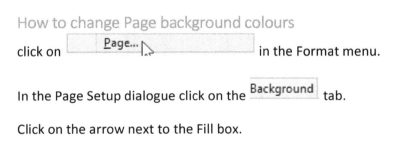

When you do this, the field which is inserted will act like a word in the text.

How to change Page background colours

click on 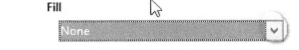 in the Format menu.

In the Page Setup dialogue click on the Background tab.

Click on the arrow next to the Fill box.

Fill

None

Chose the colour from the list

53

Fill

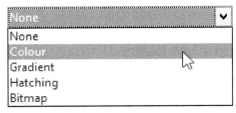

Select the appropriate colour

If you change Background settings for all pages (Yes) all the slides will be set to the colour you just changed. If you select No only the current page will be affected.

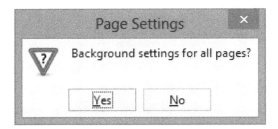

How to make a presentation Black and White or Greyscale

It can be useful to see a presentation in Black and White or Greyscale (for example, when you want to see what it'll look like on your printer).

Simply click onto a slide in the main viewable area. Then hover your mouse over Colour / Greyscale in the view menu.

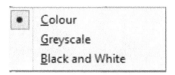

Click on Greyscale or Black and White. Then, when you're done and want to return to the colour view click on Colour.

Next Chapter

In this chapter I've shown you the basic things you'll use in almost any slide you make:

- How to insert and format text objects
- How to insert, resize and move image object
- How to chose a slide design.

With this information and the content of the last chapter you can make almost any slideshow you're likely to need.

The next chapter will describe entire slideshows.

4 SLIDESHOWS

So far we've discussed how to create slides that have impact. In this section we'll look at how to create new slides, and how to put slides into the order you'll present them.

- How to insert, delete and move slides
- Transition effects between slides
- How to animate objects in a presentation
- How to run a presentation
- How to rehearse timings
- Automatic transitions between slides
- How to create a custom slideshow
- Running the slideshow

We've already run a basic slideshow in the first chapter. While this chapter will cover some of the same ground it will go into a lot more detail.

How to insert, delete and move slides

When working with slides you'll use the Slides Dockable window on the left hand side of the screen most often.

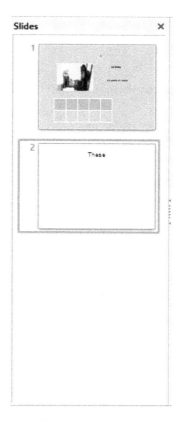

This Dockable window provides a simple interface to move, insert, delete and duplicate slides. Each slide is numbered for convenience; the numbers change as you edit the slideshow.

Inserting a new, blank slide

In the Slides Dockable window right click on the slide that will be before the slide you're about to insert. For example if you want to insert between 1 and 2 in the above example right click on slide 1.Then click

 .

Duplicating an existing slide

Right click on the slide you want to duplicate. Then click on

Duplicate Slide . You can then move the slide to the correct

place in the slideshow (see below for details)

Inserting slides from a file

In the Slides Dockable window right click on the slide that will be before

the slide you want to insert. Then click on in the Insert menu.

An Insert File dialogue will open. Chose the directory that contains the file that you want to insert, and double click on it. You'll see an Insert Slides/Object dialogue.

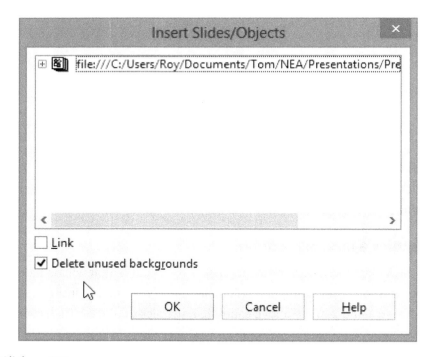

Click on OK.

If you have slides in the file that you don't want in your presentation you'll have to delete them manually. See below for information on how to do that.

Selecting a slide to work on

Click on the slide you want to edit in the Slides Dockable Window. If you have more slides that LibreOffice can display on the screen you may have to scroll down to get to the slide.

You'll see the slide you want to edit appear in the Main Viewable area.

Delete a slide

Right click on the slide you want to delete in the Slides Dockable Window. You may have to scroll to get to the slide that you want. Click .

Move a slide

Click and hold on the slide you want to move in the Slide Dockable Window. Move the mouse up or down to move the slide. You'll see a tiny slide that will indicated where you're moving the slide currently:

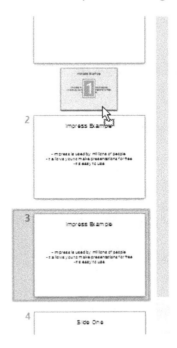

By moving the mouse to the top or bottom of the Dockable window you'll scroll up or down the screen.

When you're happy with the position of the Slide let go of the mouse. If you change your mind press the right mouse button.

Transition effects between slides

A transition is a graphical effect that happens when you go from one slide to another in a slideshow. For example "Wipe Left" which makes it appear like the slide is being swiped to the left. It's easy to change the transition for a slide in LibreOffice Impress.

First, select the slide you want in the Slides Dockable window. Once you're editing the correct slide click on

 in the Slideshow menu.

At the Bottom right hand side of the screen you'll see the Slide Transition Dockable window where the Properties Dockable Window often is:

Chose the transition you want to use:

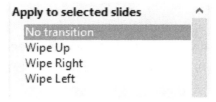

You can change how fast the transition works by clicking on the speed box,  and selecting one of the speeds from the drop down list. You can also add a sound if you want to

Sound: No Sound .

You may have to scroll down in the Transitions Dockable window to see all the options mentioned here.

To see whether your choices are what you want press Play and it will preview the transition. You can then either chose to apply the changes to the current slide by clicking on Apply to All Slides . Otherwise your choices will only apply to the current slide. Clicking on Slide Show will run the slide show so you'll be able to see what the transitions look like.

Finally, click on the properties icon (on the right of the Transitions Dockable window) to return the Transitions Dockable window to the Properties Dockable window which is the default.

NOTE:

if you change your mind about the changes to the Properties Dockable window and press the undo icon on the taskbar.

How to animate objects in a presentation

In the same way that you can use transitions between slides to make a slideshow seem more appealing, you can also animate objects on a slide.

To do this, first go to the slide that has the object or element that you want to animate. Then select the object by clicking on it.

Impress Example

Click on  in the slideshow menu.

You'll see the Custom Animation Dockable window where the property Dockable window is normally located (in the bottom right hand corner of the screen). Often you'll have to scroll down to click on the add

animation icon [⊕] . This will open the Add Animation dialogue:

There are several tabs that you can choose from. Entrance are the effects that happen when you go into the slide in the slideshow. Emphasis are ways that you can emphasise the element during the presentation, and exit are the effects that happen when you leave the slideshow to go onto the next slide. Motion Paths make the object move in a certain direction such as an arc or polygon. Misc are effects that haven't otherwise been classified.

Entrance and Exist effects happen automatically; the other classes of effects only happen when you click the object you've decided to animate unless you change the Start property in the Custom Animation Dockable window.

When you click on an effect you get a preview of what the effect looks like.

You can also change how quickly the effect works once you've selected one by changing the speed $\underline{S}$peed: [Medium ∨].

Click on Cancel if you change your mind, or OK if you're happy with your selection.

As a rule I suggest only animating the most important item on a slide. Often even that is too much and you'd only want to animate a few items in an entire presentation. Otherwise these effects can become very distracting.

Once you've finished adding Animations, click on [icon] to return the Custom Animation Dockable window into the Properties Dockable window.

How to run a presentation

Press F5 to start a presentation from the first slide, or Shift+F5 to start it from the current slide you've selected in the Slides Dockable Window.

Alternatively, click on 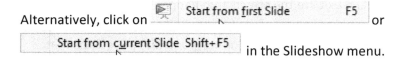 or

| Start from current Slide Shift+F5 | in the Slideshow menu.

Unless you've set up automatic timing you'll need to click on the background of a slide to move it to the next slide.

Click the black space to the left of the slide to go back a slide.

How to rehearse timings

Once you're happy with a slideshow you might want to rehearse timings. This allows you to work out how long you need for each slide in the slideshow. Click on [Rehearse Timings] in the slideshow menu.

Note that if you've got any animation effects that depend on clicking in a slide the timings won't start until those effect are finished.

At the bottom of the screen you'll see a timer . Simply do your presentation and record the amount of time that each slide takes.

Automatic transitions between slides

Once you've rehearsed the timings of the slideshow it's easy to set up automatic transitions.

First, select the slide in the Slides Dockable window. Remember that if you select slide 1, you're going to control how long slide 1 remains on the screen before the transition.

Click on Slide Transition... in the slideshow menu.

In the bottom right hand corner of the screen where the properties Dockable window is often located, you'll see the Slide Transition Dockable window.

Scroll down until you see Automatically after 1.00sec.

Click on the to toggle the option on, then enter the amount of time in the box Automatically after 5.00sec.

You could click Apply to All Slides if you want the same time for each slide but I recommend working out custom timings in which case you'd repeat the process by selecting the next slide and changing the time.

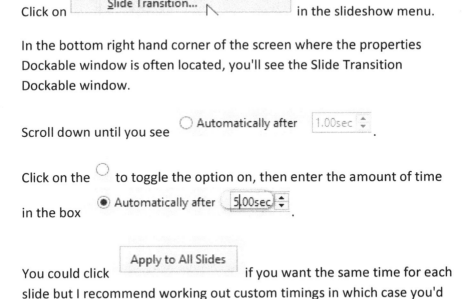

Once you've finished, click to check that your timings

are correct and adjust as necessary. When you're happy, click on
to return to the Properties Dockable window.

How to create a custom slideshow

Sometimes you may want to customise a slideshow for a particular
audience. For example, you may have a thirty minute presentation but
another audience only wants a fifteen minute presentation. You can
produce these custom slide shows easily by clicking

on  in the Slideshow menu.

This will display the Custom Slide Shows dialogue:

Click on 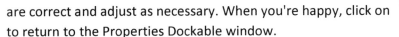 to Create a custom slideshow.

You'll see the Define Custom Slide Show. Type in a name :

Name: New Custom Slide Show

Then select a slide you want in the slideshow, and click 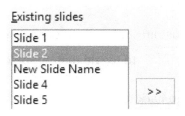 for example if you want Slide 2 in your slideshow:

Existing slides

| Slide 1 |
| Slide 2 |
| New Slide Name |
| Slide 4 |
| Slide 5 |

> >

Once you've clicked on it will appear on the custom list:

Keep on selecting slides in the order you want them to appear. If you

make a mistake select the slide you don't want, and click .

If you want to change the order of slides in the custom slide show you can drag them up or down the list by clicking the left mouse button and moving it up or down then letting it go when you're happy. You can have slides in any order:

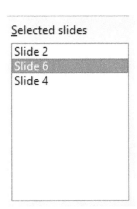

Selected slides

| Slide 2 |
| Slide 6 |
| Slide 4 |

Once you're happy click OK. If you change your mind click cancel.

You'll see the new slide show on the list in the Custom Slide Shows dialogue. Select a custom slide show and click on 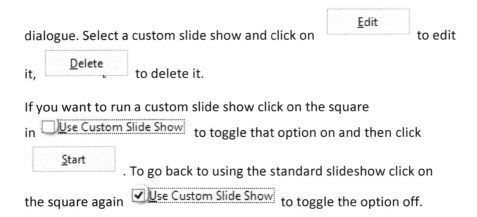 to edit it, to delete it.

If you want to run a custom slide show click on the square in to toggle that option on and then click . To go back to using the standard slideshow click on the square again to toggle the option off.

Next Chapter

In this chapter I've shown you how to use slideshows, how to time them, control transitions, and make new slides.

The next chapter will discuss how to draw on a slide.

5 DRAWING SHAPES

Shapes can be squares, text, callouts, pie charts and any number of other objects which are used to improve the look of documents.

The draw functions are generally at the bottom left hand of the viewable area:

But sometimes you might not see them since it's possible to suppress them in LibreOffice. If you don't see them , hover your mouse over toolbars and look for Drawing | Drawing | click on it, and the Drawing Toolbar should appear.

There are a lot of different Drawing tools to learn.

Here's a basic list of them:

Icon	Icon Name	Description
	Select	Select items in drawing
	Line	Add a straight line to a drawing
	Rectangle	Add a rectangle to a drawing; the rectangle can be filled
	Ellipse	Add an ellipse to a drawing; the ellipse can be filled with a colour
	Free-from line	Add a free-form (i.e. wiggly) line to a drawing
	Text	Add text
	Callouts	Add a callout - something used to label or bring attention to a part of a drawing.
	Basic Shapes	Used to insert basic shapes like triangles, squares and donuts in the drawing.
	Symbol Shapes	Add symbols like square brackets into the drawing.
	Block Arrows	Add arrows to the drawing
	Flowcharts	Insert flowchart symbols into the drawing (a flow chart is a particular type of diagram)
	Callouts	Add one of many more elaborate callouts to the drawing
	Stars	Add a star to the drawing
	Points	Points allow you to resize, change the alignment or rotate an image. You've seen them before. This icon comes on automatically when you've selected a image.
	Fontwork Gallery	Examples of fontwork. Not advised.
	From File	Add an image from a file.
	Extrusion On/Off	Switched 3D effect on for image. When you put on Extrusion you'll see a number of other icons added to the draw bar.

Insert a Line

Inserting a line is simple. You click on the line icon, ╱ , press and hold the left mouse button at the place on the slide you want the line to start, move the mouse to the end of the line and let go.

But, after you've done that you see some interesting new icons on the taskbar:

To make the line into an arrow

Click on the ▾ next to ⇇ ▾ to show a list of arrows:

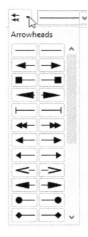

and click on the arrowhead style that you want.

Change the style, and size of the line

Next to the Arrow icon there are boxes to determine the line style (1) and Line width (2).

To change the line style(icon 1) click on it, and you will see a list of possible line styles.

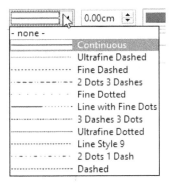

Click on the one you want. You can also change the width by clicking on 2 and typing in a width, _____ or clicking on the up (to increase the width) ▲ or down ▼ arrows.

Change the colour of the line

Next to the width box is the Line Colour box _____ . Click on it to show the colour selection dialogue and click on the colour you want.

Moving object behind / in front of other objects

An object is in front of another object if it obscures the other object. So, in this example the Box is behind the text:

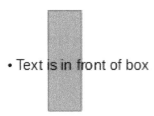

• Text is in front of box

And in this example the box is in front of the text:

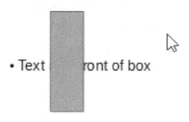

• Text front of box

To send an object behind another object, right click on the object and hover your mouse over Arrange and click on Send to Back . To bring it in front hover your mouse over Arrange and click on Bring to Front . If you've got multiple objects you can arrange them further using the send forwards and send backwards options, but I don't recommend having that many objects in the same place in a slide since this can be confusing. If you're using that many objects I recommend using a drawing program and inserting the final image.

Some other thoughts

Things like lines, rectangles, and other shapes are images in LibreOffice so the methods I've already shown you when we were dealing with images such as how to rotate, resize, and wrap work in the same way I've described earlier.

I don't want to bore you by repeatedly describing the same action; in the descriptions below it's assumed that things that are common behaviour for shapes will work as you expect it unless I specify otherwise.

Rectangles

Press the rectangle icon and move your mouse to the top left of the new rectangle. Press and hold the mouse button down, then move diagonally to the bottom right of the rectangle.

A rectangle can be divided into a line (i.e. the border around the rectangle) and a fillable area (i.e. the solid colour inside the line).

You've already seen how to change the thickness, style and colour of a line. You can use these options on the rectangle too, for e.g.

Changing the Fill style and Fill colour of the area

You'll find the Area Style (1) and Filling (2) next to Line Colour on the taskbar.

Click on Area Style(1) to select whether you want to fill the area with colour, a gradient, hatching or a bitmap.

Once you've selected that, click on Filling (2) to chose the filling you want, for example

would produce the following box:

It's worth playing around with the options to see what's available.

Adding Text to a shape

You'll often want to add text to a shape. Simply double click on the centre of the shape, and enter in your text. Once you've finished, click off the Rectangle (i.e. on an empty spot elsewhere on the document).You'll quickly notice that there's something odd about it:

then Right click on the rectangle, and select Text:

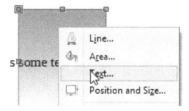

In the Text Dialogue you will see an option to Word Wrap. Click it.

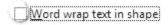

Then select OK.

When you're editing text you will see that the draw icons have been replaced by text icons in the taskbar. You can change font, size, add emphasis italics and bold just like normal:

Insert a Ellipse

Insert an ellipse by clicking on the Ellipse icon ⬭ and then move your mouse to the top right hand corner of an imaginary rectangle

75

surrounding your ellipse. Click and hold the mouse, moving it to the bottom right hand corner.

Select multiple Drawing Objects

So far I've ignored one icon. The Select icon. . Hold down the shift and click on each drawing object that you want to select.

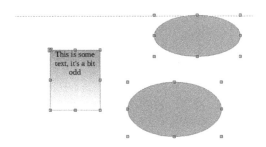

Grouping multiple Drawing Objects

It's possible to combine multiple images so they act like they are all one image - in other words you can move them or resize them as a group instead of having to treat each image separately.

Once you've selected all the images (see above) right click on one and select Group

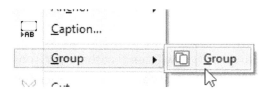

If you want to split the group apart again, right click and select Ungroup.

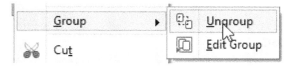

Sometimes you may want to edit an item in the group individually, but

not lose the fact it's in a group once you've finished editing it. Select Edit Group. Once you've edited the group, click off somewhere empty in the document.

Free Form Line

If you want to make a wriggly line LibreOffice has a tool just for you. Click on the arrow next to the curves icon (note, this can be found to the

right of the Text icon on the draw toolbar) and select freeform

line . Move the mouse to the beginning of the line you're drawing. Click and hold down the mouse, then draw the line you want. Let go when you've finished.

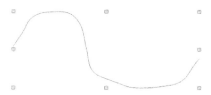

If you want to edit the path of the line click on the Points icon . You will see the line now has points all the way along it:

If you click on one of the points you will see two circle either side of a black square:

If you click on and move the Black square the actual path of the line will change between the adjacent two rectangles making a large change:

If you click and move the circle, you only affect the line between two rectangles:

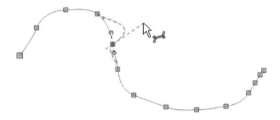

There are many other types of curves that you can add. It's worth trying them out to see how they work.

How to Rotate objects

Right click on the object that you want to rotate and then click on ⊡ Position and Size... . You'll see the position and size dialogue. There's a Default settings option.

Default settings

Click on the round circle at the end of the line , hold the mouse button down and then move clockwise or counter clockwise letting go of the mouse when you're at the correct angle.

Click on OK when you're happy.

Shapes

LibreOffice allows you to add a lot of shapes into a diagram. Shapes are pre-created draw objects that you can use to improve the look of you document. We've already described some basic shapes - rectangles and ellipses.

LibreOffice offers several categories of shapes on the draw toolbox by default including Basic Shapes(1), Symbol Shapes (2), Block Arrows (3), Flowchart (4), callouts (5) and stars (6). Your installation of LibreOffice may have different icons on the toolbar. This is because it's possible to add or remove categories from the toolbar.

You can see shapes that are less commonly used by right clicking the bar on the left of the draw toolbox   and then hovering your mouse over

Visible Buttons ▶. You will see a list of icons; some are highlighted out, some aren't. If you click on a type of shape that is not highlighted you'll see that type of shape appear in the draw toolbar. If you click on a type of shape that is highlighted it'll disappear from the draw toolbar.

In the above diagram clicking on Free-Form line would remove it from the draw toolbar. Clicking on Curve would add it to the draw toolbar.

Once you've added the class of shape you want to the draw toolbar (if it isn't there already!) you can choose to insert the default form of that shape by clicking on its icon. For example, for the basic block arrow click on ⬄▾ . You draw the shape onto the screen in the same way you'd draw a text box or callout.

Sometimes there are multiple versions of a shape. You can tell that there are variations available because there will be a down arrow next ▾ next to the icon for the shape type you want. Click on it to select a variation. For example, to choose a variation of a block arrow click on ⬄▾.You'll see a large gallery of block arrows to choose from:

Click on the type of block arrow that that you want. You can then insert it in the same way you'd insert a rectangle.

It's easy to add another arrow of the same type because LibreOffice changes the default to the most recently inserted variation of a shape. So, after I insert a right arrow, the block arrow item in the drawbar

changes to and you'd just hit the highlighted portion for another right arrow.

Curves

Click on the down arrows in the Curves icon which you can find

to the right of the Text icon. Click on . To create a curve, move the mouse pointer to the start of the curve on the screen, click and hold the left mouse button. Move to the end of the line, let go of the mouse button. Now, move the mouse in the direction you want the image to curve. Double click when you're happy with the curve.

Note: It is possible to draw more than one curve or straight line at a time but I don't recommend doing this since it can be very temperamental. Instead, group a collection of lines and curves together to make the shape you want.

Making some shapes 3D

Sometimes you might want to make a shape 3D. While you can't do this to some drawing objects such as lines, arcs, or rectangles, LibreOffice does offer it for other types of shapes (including those from the basic shape gallery, ellipses gallery etc).

If you select a shape by left clicking it you'll see a greyed out Extrusion

On/Off icon if you can't add a 3D effect to that shape. If you can

add a 3D effect the Extrusion icon will be in full colour . Clicking on it will give the object a basic 3D effect but it'll also add some icons to the draw toolbar:

Extrusion On/Off

Click this item to remove the 3d effect

Tilt Icons

Click these to tilt the shape Down(1), Up(2), Left(3) and Right(4).

Depth

Click this to change the depth of the 3d effect. LibreOffice shows a list of options. If one of them is OK for you click on it.

Otherwise, clicking on custom allows you to specify exactly how deep the 3d effect should be.

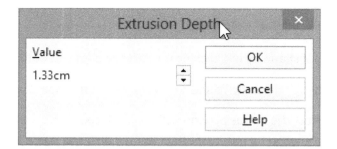

Direction

Although you can control the direction of the 3D effect using the Tilt options described above there are some standard ways to display perspective available using the direction icon. Click on the one that you want:

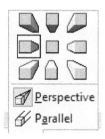

Lighting

Depending on the Lighting direction your 3D effect will display shadows in different places. Click on the icon and it will show you a list of lighting directions:

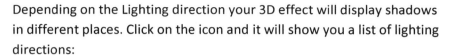

Click on the bulb determine which is the brightest side of the object. You can also change how light or dim it is, although I recommend keeping this on normal.

Surface

Click on this and you'll have the option of different surface types. In theory you can use this to change the look of the surface but the only one I find really changes much is the Wire Frame option which can be quite useful.

3D Colour

This allows you to change the colour of the 3D portion of the shape. When you click on it you'll see a colour selection dialogue. Pick one.

You'll notice that the colour you've selected will be altered by the lighting option you chose above - so portions in shade will be lighter than the colour you selected, and portions in shadow will be darker:

Next Chapter

In this chapter I've shown you how to use the Draw toolbar to add shapes, images, and adjust them. These functions - although not as sophisticated as a full desktop publishing program - allow you to make very nice looking slides.

The next chapter I'll describe how to add other types of objects.

6 OBJECTS

In this chapter I'm going to explain about more types of objects, including:

- Table objects
- Chart Objects
- Movie and Sound objects
- OLE Objects

These objects allow you to enhance a presentation quite considerably.

Table objects
Tables are typically used to present data clearly and simply.

Inserting a table

To insert a table click on the down arrow next to the table icon on the

taskbar . You'll see a grid of squares

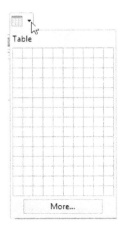

By bringing your mouse down into the grid you can tell LibreOffice how many columns and rows you want in your table. The grid will fill up with blue squares in the shape of the table you are going to insert:

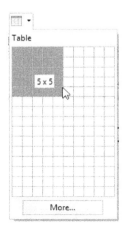

LibreOffice also writes the size of the table you're going to insert. A 2 x 4 table has two columns and four rows. Click on the right hand corner square of your table. LibreOffice will insert a table into your slide:

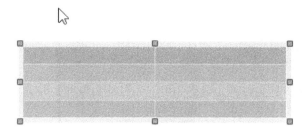

Resizing and moving a table

You can resize the table by clicking on the border and using the blue rectangles like any other object. Moving a table is accomplished by clicking and holding on the border of the table and then dragging the table to the right place on the slide.

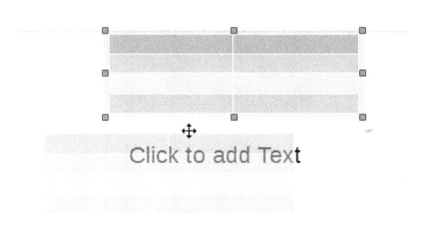

Resizing a row or column

But you may also want to change the width or length of a row.

To do this hover your mouse over the line that denotes the cell boundary e.g.

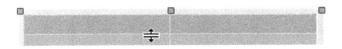

Then click and hold the left mouse button and move it to the place you want it to go. This can be tricky and takes a little bit of practice.

Entering data

Click on the cell you want to add data to. The cursor will appear and you'll be able to add text just like a text box.

Inserting a row or column

Right Click on a cell in the row or column next to the one you want to insert. Hover your mouse over Row (or column, if appropriate) and click Insert.

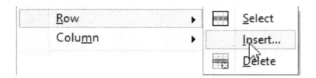

The insert row dialogue gives you the opportunity to choose how many rows to add

and also chose whether to add the row above (before) or below (after) the row you right clicked on.

Click OK when you're happy. This, for example, is the result of selecting inserting a row after row 1:

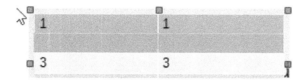

You can insert a column in the same way (although you would hover your mouse over column and not row)

Right clicking on the row and clicking on row->Delete will delete the row. row->Select will select the row.

The same holds true for columns, although you would use column->Select or Column->Delete.

Formatting a table

You can select multiple cells by clicking on the bottom right hand corner of your selection, holding the mouse down, and moving the mouse to

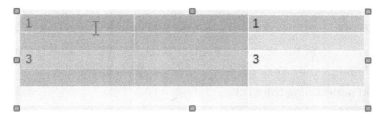

the top left hand corner of the table.

Select all the cells you want to format, then right click and on the highlighted (blue) area and click on [Table...] .

You'll see a Properties dialogue that initially allows you to select fonts.

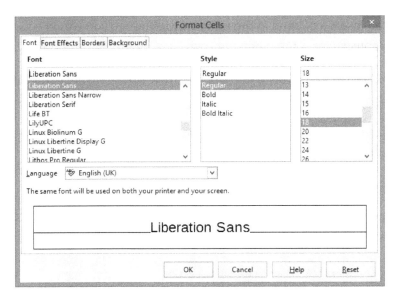

Clicking on the tab at the top allows you to also adjust font effects (such as bold and italic), the cell borders (removing cell lines) and the background (controlling the colour).

Chart Objects

To insert a chart click on the chart icon ☁ in the taskbar.

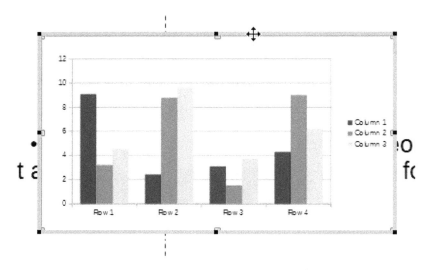

You can move and resize a chart in the same way as any other object -

to move hover the mouse pointer over the chart's boundary until it changes to , click and hold the left mouse button and drop it where you want the object on the screen. To resize, click on the boundary and then click on one of the rectangles on the edges of the object in the same way you'd resize a text box.

When inserting a chart LibreOffice will only insert the default chart type - often a bar chart. To select what type of chart you want click on the chart, and you'll see the chart taskbar appear:

Click on the chart type icon .

The Chart Type dialogue will appear. On the left of the screen you see different types of charts that you can insert:

Click on one to select that type of chart. Each type of chart has several instances, for example if you click on line, you'd see:

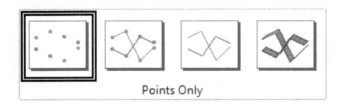

Points Only

Select the instance that you want the chart to look like. Below the instances you'll often see relevant options of the particular type of chart. If you were to select a bar chart, for example, you can add a 3d look e.g. choosing Cone gives you a range of cone options

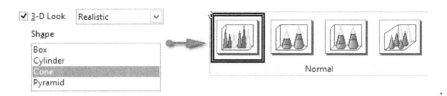

Once you're happy, click OK.

Changing data in a table

So far all we have is a generic, default chart with no useful data.

Pressing the chart data table icon ⊡ will display the Chart Data Table dialogue which allows you to customise the data in the table.

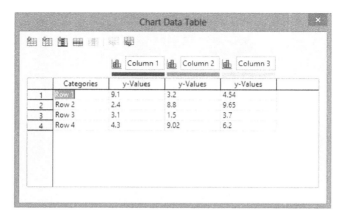

Note that by clicking on the column boxes 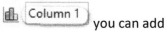 you can add a name to each column, e.g.

changes the chart so the blue column is called Name 1.

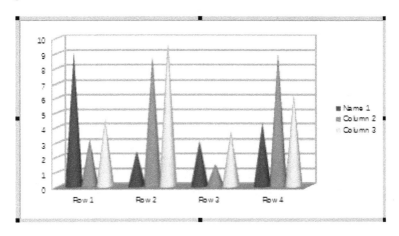

You can change the category by clicking onto the appropriate row and changing the name:

	Categories	y-Values	y-Values	y-Val ies
1	My First categor	9.1	3.2	4.54
2	Row 2	2.4	8.8	9.65
3	My third categoi	3.1	1.5	3.7
4	Row 4	4.3	9.02	6.2

Produces the following chart:

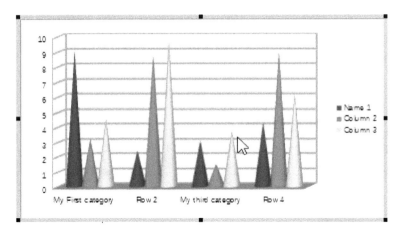

And of course you can change the data just the same as any cell by clicking in the first box in the sequence, editing the cell, then tabbing to the next box and so on.

...	...	...	...
My third categoi	2	1	0

Produces:

My third category

To insert a row, click on the row just above where you want the row to be inserted, and click insert row .

To delete a row, click on the row you want deleted, and then click the delete row icon .

To delete a series, (i.e. the numbers under a column) click onto the series and then click the delete series icon .

To insert a series, click to the left of where you want the series to be inserted, and then click the insert series icon . This icon is hard to distinguish, see below for the location:

To move a row down, click on any cell on the row and then click on the move row down icon ⬛ . To move a series right, click on any cell in the series and then click on the move series right icon ⬛ . Once you click OK, the chart.

Changing the colour of a series

You may want to change the colour associated with a series. Double click on an object in the series on the chart. Click on the Area tab, then select the colour you want for the series:

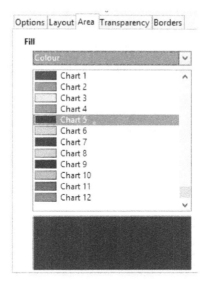

Adding a title to the chart

Right click on an empty area of the chart, and then click

.

You'll see the Titles dialogue.

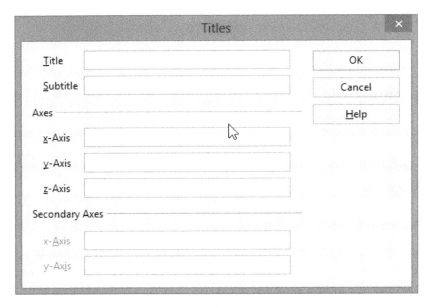

You can insert a main title, and title for the Axes, i.e.

<u>T</u>itle	My Main titile
<u>S</u>ubtitle	A subtitle

Axes

<u>x</u>-Axis	LibreAccess
<u>y</u>-Axis	Impress

You'll notice that the font is often very small on the titles. Right click on the title, and click on <u>F</u>ormat Title... . You'll be able to change the size of the title, and put in effects like italic and bold. You can also do the same thing to legends, subtitles, and axes.

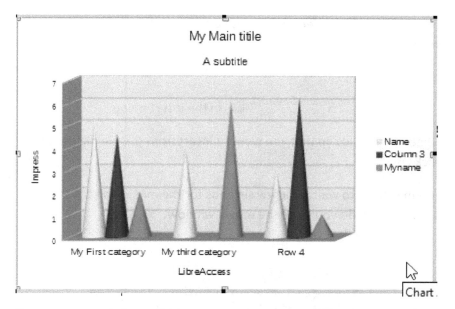

Charts are especially useful in presentations. LibreOffice does provide basic chart facilities but it also gives you the ability to insert OLE objects like excel documents which seriously enhances the basic LibreOffice chart facilities. I'll give you a short rundown of that later on in the chapter.

Sound objects

Click on  in the insert menu.

Select the music or sound clip that you want to insert from the file dialogue and click OK.

You'll see the sound object appear in your slide

When you are viewing the slideshow and get to that slide the sound will start to play automatically.

To delete a sound object simply click on it and hit the delete key on your keyboard.

Movie objects

Click on 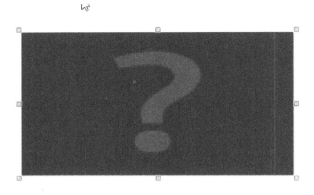 in the insert menu.

Select the movie clip that you want to insert from the file dialogue and click OK.

You may have to wait for a few seconds for the movie object to load, but when you do you'll see the movie window.

You can move or resize the window like normal.

When you get to the slide you've put the movie object on it'll start playing immediately.

To delete a movie object simply click on it and hit the delete key on your keyboard.

Insert an OLE Object

LibreOffice allows you to insert all kinds of objects into your document. These objects include LibreOffice Writer documents, charts, and objects from other programs such as Microsoft word documents.

Hover your mouse over Objects in the insert menu and click OLE Object.

If it's a standard LibreOffice object double click on it:

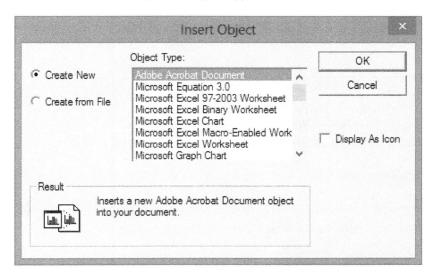

If it's an object from another program, double click on

Further objects

You'll see a the insert object dialogue appear:

You can chose to double click on one of the Object types if you want to create a new object of that type. The program will open up and allow you to create a document or object of that type. When you save and close the program any changes you've made will appear in a relevant object on the slideshow

You can also chose to insert an object from a file.

Click on the round circle next to Create from File . You'll see a file, and a browse buttons.

File:
C:\Users\Roy\Documents\Tom\NEA\
Browse...

Click on Browse and you'll see a browse dialogue. Go to the correct directory and select the file you want to insert as an OLE object.

LibreOffice may take a little while to think things through, so be patient.

You can move and resize OLE objects like any other object, and delete them by clicking on them and pressing the delete key.

Obviously, this is a very powerful facility since you can access many of the best features of a range of software programs within LibreOffice. I've just touched the surface of what you can do with it in this section. It's worth experimenting with when you're comfortable with the basics.

Next Chapter

In this chapter I've shown you how to include tables and charts of data as well as how to improve a presentation with sound and movies, or other document objects.

The next chapter will discuss how to edit and format slides.

7 EDITING SLIDES

In this chapter I'm going to explain how to edit slides including how to:

- Cut, copy and paste objects
- Spell Checking
- Headers and Footers
- Find & Replace
- Formatting the Screen Size

While this chapter will cover familiar ground for many of you it's still very useful stuff to know.

Cut, Copy and Paste Objects

Cut, copying and pasting objects works in a similar way to text. Right click on the object - whether it's a text box, an image, or a shape - and select either cut or copy from the menu.

Go to the slide where you want to paste the object, and right click on the slides background. Then select _____. You'll have to move the object to wherever you want it.

Spell Checking

Using automatic spell checking

By default LibreOffice Impress automatically spell checks as you type text into a textbox. When you press certain buttons such as full stop or enter LibreOffice checks the sentence for errors and underlines any potential errors in red.

This docckument hass a lot of errorss

Right clicking on a word with an error produces a list of suggestions.

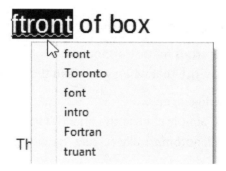

Clicking on one of the suggestions will change the word to that suggestion.

Ignore a word or Ignore all instances of a word using the automatic spell check

Sometimes you don't want LibreOffice to correct a word but you don't want to add it to the dictionary which applies to all documents. For example if you are working for a company with an unusual name.

LibreOffice allows you to ignore all instances of that word in the document by right clicking on the word and selecting

.

Before using the Ignore All feature you should make sure that the word is spelled correctly. LibreOffice won't alert you to the word again so if it's wrong it is unlikely that you will pick up the mistake.

Adding a word to the dictionary using automatic spell check

Warning: it is very important to make sure that any word you add to the dictionary is spelled correctly.

To add a word to the dictionary right click on the word and select "Add to dictionary" [Add to Dictionary]. LibreOffice will take this word to be a valid English language word (even if the word is in fact incorrect).

Always correct with automatic spell check

This is another dangerous feature although it can be useful. Say, you always accidentally write that when you mean that. Right clicking on that and then hovering over [AutoCorrect ▶] will produce a list of corrections. Simply choose the one that you want. From that point LibreOffice will automatically correct the word.

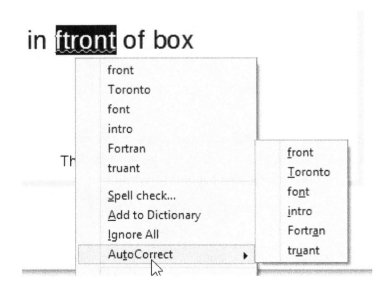

Turning off (or on) the automatic spell check

While many people like automatic spell checking other people find the existence of red underlining as they're working very distracting. If you want to turn off the automatic spell check simply click on the icon

 . You can always turn it on again by clicking on again.

How to use the Spell Check and Grammar check

While the automatic spell check is very useful many people will want to run a full spelling or grammar check because it has additional facilities.

To start the spell check press function key 7(F7) or click on spelling and grammar on the tools menu.

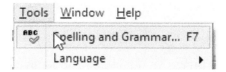

LibreOffice will display a Spelling dialogue, see below:

Text Language

The first thing you see in the Spelling dialogue is the text language that LibreOffice is checking against.

If you click on the down arrow it will provide you with a list of other languages. If the language you're writing isn't English, simply select the correct language from the list.

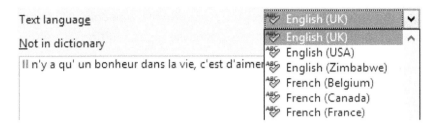

Ignore / Ignore All

Notice that the next thing you see is an error dialogue with suggestions beneath it. In this case, LibreOffice doesn't recognise the French word Il. It's suggesting the English word I.

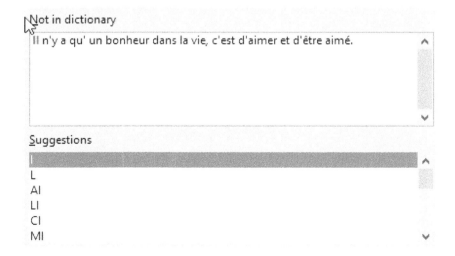

If you are happy with the word you can press 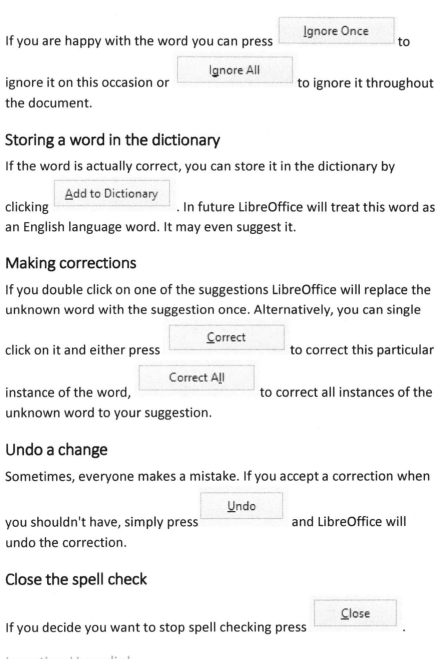 to ignore it on this occasion or to ignore it throughout the document.

Storing a word in the dictionary

If the word is actually correct, you can store it in the dictionary by clicking . In future LibreOffice will treat this word as an English language word. It may even suggest it.

Making corrections

If you double click on one of the suggestions LibreOffice will replace the unknown word with the suggestion once. Alternatively, you can single click on it and either press to correct this particular instance of the word, to correct all instances of the unknown word to your suggestion.

Undo a change

Sometimes, everyone makes a mistake. If you accept a correction when you shouldn't have, simply press and LibreOffice will undo the correction.

Close the spell check

If you decide you want to stop spell checking press .

Inserting Hyperlink

Select the text that you want to make into a hyperlink, then click on

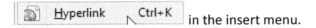 in the insert menu.

You'll see the Hyperlink dialogue.

Link to a document

You'll see a section in the dialogue called document.

Click on the Open file button (highlighted above).

An open file dialogue will display. Change the directory and select the file you want to link to, then click OK.

 to make the link if you're happy or edit the Further Settings below.

Link to Slide in Document

In the dialogue there's a section called Target in document. Click on the Target In Document icon (the circle with a dot inside it highlighted below)

an Target in Document dialogue will open up with a list of the slides in the current document.

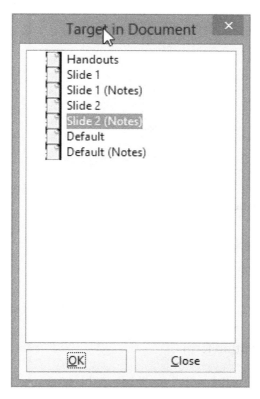

Double click on the slide that you want to link to.

Click **Apply** to make the link if you're happy or edit the Further Settings below.

Making an Internet Link

Click on **Internet** on the left of the Hyperlink dialogue.

By default it links to a web page, but you can click on the circle next to ○ FTP to link to a FTP site.

Enter the Internet Address / URL into the Target field

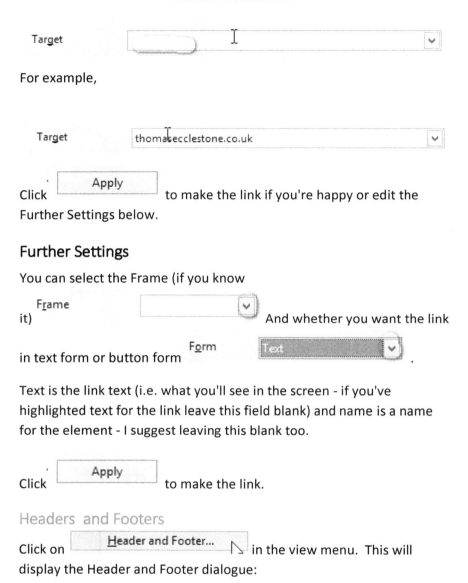

For example,

Click [Apply] to make the link if you're happy or edit the Further Settings below.

Further Settings

You can select the Frame (if you know it) And whether you want the link in text form or button form .

Text is the link text (i.e. what you'll see in the screen - if you've highlighted text for the link leave this field blank) and name is a name for the element - I suggest leaving this blank too.

Click [Apply] to make the link.

Headers and Footers

Click on [Header and Footer...] in the view menu. This will display the Header and Footer dialogue:

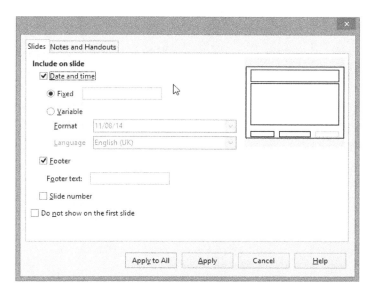

You can toggle off the date by clicking on the tick next to Date and time
✔ Date and time .

If the date is on, the default setting of fixed is used. Enter a date in the
box provided ⦿ Fixed [   ] in which case the
presentation will always show the date you entered. You can also use
today's date by clicking the round circle next to variable
○ Variable and selecting the format you want
Format [11/08/14   ∨] .

Finally, you can choose whether to add some text (for example your
name) to the footer Footer text: [   ] or toggle on
the slide number by clicking the square next to ☐ Slide number .

If you want to make the changes to all slides in the Slideshow, click
[Apply to All] . That's my recommended option. You can alter only

one slide by clicking on Apply but I recommend keeping all headers and footers the same.

There is another tab on this dialogue that is useful when you are handing out notes on the presentation. I'll describe these features at a later stage.

Find & Replace

Sometime you may want to find a phrase or sentence. Press either

Ctrl+F or  in the Edit menu .

Just above the Draw Toolbar you'll see the Find Toolbar:

Exist Search ✖

Click this icon to close the Find toolbar.

Search Phrase   It was   ⌄

Type in the phrase you are looking for here. Clicking on ⌄ will show a list of previous searches to choose from.

Find Next ⌄ Find Previous ⌃

Click on Find Next (the down arrow) to search forward in the slideshow (in other words, towards the end of the slideshow), or Find Previous to go backwards in the slideshow (towards the front) from the present location of the cursor. If you don't find anything in the direction you're searching, LibreOffice will ask if you want to start at the other end of the slideshow.

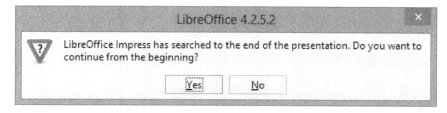

If there aren't any examples of the phrase, you'll see a message saying "Search Key Not Found."

Matching the case ☐ Match Case

By default LibreOffice matches any combination of capital and lower case letters with any other combination. So it considers It Was and iT wAS as the same phrase.

If you want to search for phrases with the exact same capitalisation, toggle the Match case option on by clicking on the ☐ to make it look like ☑ Match Case . You can click on it again to turn Match Case off.

How to Replace text

Sometimes you might decide that you want to change instances of a particular word to another one in your slideshow. For example, if you were creating a presentation about Darren and he changed his name to Danny you'd have to make a lot of changes..

To Find and Replace text either press Ctrl+H or the find and replace icon

.

This displays the Replace dialogue. You can type in your search text, then hit Find for the next instance of that search text. I find that's the best option since you don't want to replace something that matches your search text by accident!

Put the text you want to replace in the Replace With box. Click Find to find the next instance, then Replace if you want to replace the text.

As in the Find Toolbar ☐ Match case restricts the results to those phrases with identical case. Toggling on ☐ Whole words only stops LibreOffice matching partial words. For example, Tom and the first three letters of Tomorrow would match with ☐ Whole words only toggled off, but with ✔ Whole words only toggled on they won't match.

Clicking on ⊞ Other Options gives you access to some other search options that are too advanced for this book but include things like registered expressions and searching for fonts.

The Ruler

When you are designing a slide it can be useful to have an indicator of where you're putting objects and text boxes. One of the ways LibreOffice provides to give you this kind of indication is the Ruler. Click on Ruler in the view menu to see it.

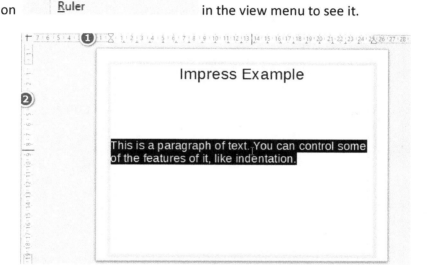

There are two rulers - a ruler for the width(1) and a ruler for the length (2) of the document.

One thing that's not immediately apparent is that as you move the mouse a bar will move on both rulers 'pointing' to the mouse.

The Grid

When you were a kid at school you'd often be given gridded paper during math class to make it easier to draw graphs or align tables on a piece of paper. The Grid words the same way.

To display the grid hover your mouse over Grid in the view menu and then click on display grid.

You'll see the grid over your slide:

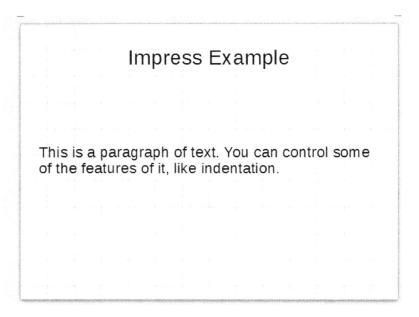

By default LibreOffice puts objects in front of the grid, but you can change this by hovering your mouse over Grid in the view menu and then clicking Grid to Front.

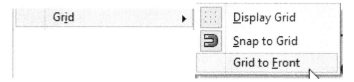

You'll see the Grid lines obscuring the objects which can be particularly noticeable with images.

Snap to grid forces objects you are moving to the nearest grid line. It helps you align objects together. You can turn it on by hovering your mouse over Grid in the view menu and then clicking on Snap to Grid.

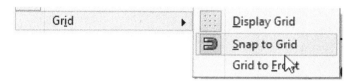

With all three of these options you can click on them a second time to toggle them off (i.e. if you have the grid showing and then click on Display Grid the grid won't be showing. If you have snap to grid on and the grid isn't showing when you move objects around they will still snap to the grid - which might make LibreOffice act in a slightly strange way!)

Snap Lines

In the same way you can choose to make objects snap to a grid you can also make lines - called snap lines - which objects will automatically align to.

First, you'll need to make LibreOffice display snap lines. Hover your mouse over Snap Lines in the view menu then click on Display Snap Lines to toggle them on.

You can make the snap lines go in front of objects by clicking on Snap Lines to Front

Making a snap line is hard to explain. If you want to make a snap line along the width of your page, move your mouse to the edge of the length ruler.

Click and hold your left mouse button, then drag your mouse towards the slide. You'll see a dotted line

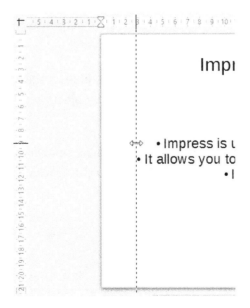

Let go when the snap line is in the correct place.

To make a snap line that separates the document in half along the length of the slide, go to the edge of the top ruler (the width ruler), click and hold then drag the mouse down.

Once you have the snap lines in the places that you want them, hover your mouse over Snap Lines in the view menu and click on Snap to Snap Lines.

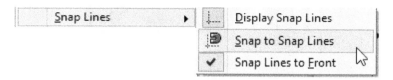

When you move an object close to the snap line it'll automatically move to the line. This makes it easier to put the line where you want it.

To remove a snap line hover your mouse over the Line. The pointer will change

Click and hold the mouse button, and drag the line to a ruler on either side of the screen (note above, the mouse pointer actually has arrows showing which direction to move it). When the snap line is on the ruler let go.

Formatting the Slides Screen Size

Click on Page... in the Format menu. You'll see the Page Format dialogue.

While you can specify custom width and height measurements I generally suggest clicking the down arrow next too format.

This produces a scrollable list of options. Click on the Format you want. Normally, that will be one of the "Screen" size format such as Screen 4:3, Screen 16:9, or Screen 16:10.

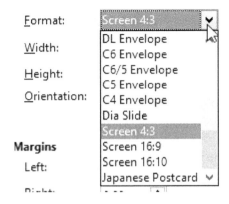

Next Chapter

In this chapter I've described some useful features for editing slides, including changing the screen format, cut and pasting, spell checking and find and replace.

The next chapter will show you how to create handouts, notes, and also how to export the files you produce to PowerPoint format and how to print out slideshows.

8 VIEWS

So far all the presentations we've produced have been shown on screen. While that's a great start people often like printed notes with their presentations.

This chapter will describe:

- The notes slide view
- The handout slide view
- The Outline view
- How to print a presentation
- How to export a presentation to other formats including PDF
- How to save a presentation to PowerPoint format
- How to Zoom in the document
- How to use the Slide Navigator

Basic information about Views

Just above the Slide you'll see a tab with different views:

So far we've been working in Normal View. However, LibreOffice Impress provides you with some other views that can be useful when you want to do particular things.

For example, the Outline view gives you a list of slide titles and contents:

Impress Example
- Impress is used by millions of people all at once
- It allows you to make presentations for free

Using LibreOffice
- Start by installing
- Then create a slide show

Presentation
Show the Presentation by pressing F5

Which is a useful way of condensing the information you're working on.

The notes view allows you to write notes about the contents of a slide, and the handout view allows you to produce handouts of the slideshow for people who have attended it.

The Outline view

To open the Outline View click on Outline in the view tab above the slide. The slide you're working on will be replaced by an outline of the presentation:

The slide you're working on at the moment is highlighted.

You can click onto the text on any slide and edit it for example clicking after installing:

₂ Using LibreOffice
- Start by installing
- Then create a slide show

and then adding some text. If you press enter you'll insert a new line:

₂ Using LibreOffice
- Start by installing LibreOffice
- Then Create your Slideshow
- Then create a slide show

As you edit the text, the slides Dockable window will change giving you a preview of the changes you're making to the presentation.

The Outline view is particularly useful when you're editing the slideshow as a whole, making sure that the sum is more than the parts.

The notes slide view

The notes slide view allows you to write notes to go with each slide in the presentation. Often you might do a presentation only once or twice a year and notes can help to record your thoughts about topics that you might become rusty on.

Alternatively, if you're doing a presentation and you might want to provide references to students, or more detailed information about some of your points the Notes view might be useful.

To get into the notes view click on Notes at the top of the main viewable area (often above the slide, or the outline).

The notes view consists of the slide, and then a section to add notes. You can't edit the slide in the Notes view it is their simply to show you what is on the slide.

Click where it says "Click to add notes" then add your notes.

The handout slide view

Often you want to give copies of slides to people that attended the presentation. But a slide can take up a lot of space on a piece of paper. LibreOffice gives you an option called "Handouts" that prints a number of slides on each piece of paper.

The handout view allows you to control the appearance of these handouts. Click on Handout in the views tab.

You'll see a preview of the current handout style showing the header and footer and number of slides:

The most important part of this view is in the Properties Dockable window. You can choose how many slides to show at once. The default of six slides can be too many for some presentations. Simply click on the handout style you want.

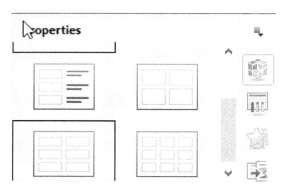

You can scroll up or down to find other numbers of slides.

How to print a presentation

While you can press the Print File Directly icon 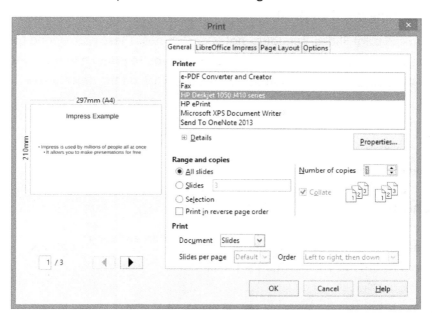 in the taskbar, I find
that it's better to press Ctrl+P or click on 🖶 Print...   Ctrl+P
in the File menu to produce the Print dialogue.

Chose printer

In the Printer dialogue you'll see Printer as the first item. Check that the
highlighted printer in the list is the one that you want to print to.
Otherwise (if necessary) scroll down the list and click on the printer that
you want to print to.

Printer

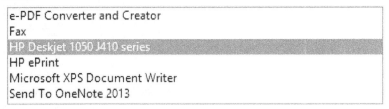

Choosing what to print

You can print Slides, handouts, notes or Outlines. These correspond to the view I talked about earlier. Check which you're printing in the Print section. If you're not printing the right thing click on the down arrow

and chose the right option from the list.

Chose which pages to Print

Once you've chosen what to print, set the **Range and copies** options next. By default you normally print all slides

But if you click on the circle by 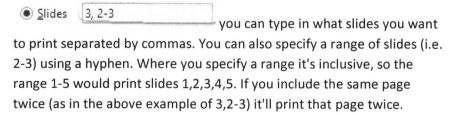 you'll print the slide you're working on at the moment, and if you click on the circle by

you can type in what slides you want to print separated by commas. You can also specify a range of slides (i.e. 2-3) using a hyphen. Where you specify a range it's inclusive, so the range 1-5 would print slides 1,2,3,4,5. If you include the same page twice (as in the above example of 3,2-3) it'll print that page twice.

You can also edit the number in to alter the

number of printouts you'll print.

Finally, check the print preview on the left hand of the screen to make sure you're printing what you want to print.

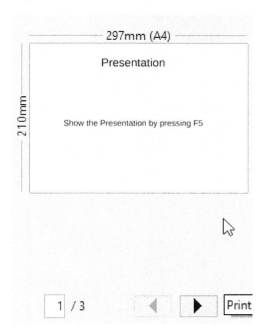

If you need to change printer properties such as the paper size or orientation of the pages you're printing see the next section.

Otherwise, click OK to print.

Printer Properties

If you need to set printer properties click on the

 button in the Print dialogue.

Orientation is the direction of the paper. Portrait is where the shortest length is parallel with the floor

By clicking on the Portrait you can change it to landscape

You can also set how many pages per sheet, which can be useful when printing slides. When printing outlines, notes or handouts I think it's best not to use this option.

If you need to change the paper size click on Advanced... and then the down arrow next to the paper format. Where you want to change an option in this dialogue you may have to click on the underline section

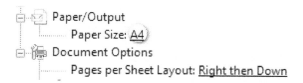

This produces a list box where you can select the option you want.

Click OK in the advanced dialogue when you're happy, then OK in the Document Properties window. You'll return to the Print Dialogue where you can print out if you want to.

How to export a presentation PDF

Press the export directly icon in the taskbar. You'll see a save file dialogue open. Change the filename and directory as appropriate then click ok.

If you want more control over the export process you can also click on Export as PDF... in the File menu. This shows a dialogue with a lot more options but I find that I'm perfectly happy with exporting directly and it's a simpler way to do things.

How to export a presentation to other file formats

Click on Export... in the File menu.

You'll get a export dialogue. Chose the filename and dialogue, and click on the Save as type.

Select the export type that you want and click OK.

While this is often OK, sometimes there will be a file type that you want to export to but which isn't supported by this dialogue. An example is the PowerPoint format. See below for more detail about how to export to a format like that.

How to save a presentation to PowerPoint format

Which export provides you a way of producing files in other computer program formats where there is no risk of formatting errors, there are some platforms where LibreOffice can save in the format but you may lose a certain amount of design or formatting data. Power Point format is one example of this.

While that sounds bad, the reality is that almost always saving as a file works completely smoothly and is as good as "Exporting" a file.

Press  in the File menu.

Use the dialogue as a normal Save dialogue setting the filename and directory as normal.

Then click on the arrow next to save as type:

You'll see a list of types you can save as. Click on the one that you want to use, for example Microsoft PowerPoint 2007/2010/2013 XML.

Then click save.

How to Zoom in the document

Sometimes you may want to make the slide you're working on appear bigger or smaller. Hover your mouse over  in the view menu.

You'll see a list of zoom options - click on different ones to see what they do.

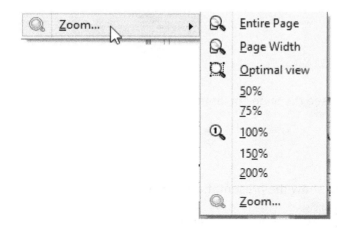

I find that Optimal View is often the best one to use, but sometimes I like to use 100% to get a feel of what the slide will really look like when I'm actually showing it. Particularly when I'm working with images.

Slide Sorter View

While so far in this chapter I've discussed the most commonly used views - Outline, notes and slide - the Slide Sorter view can be useful when combined with the Slide Navigator.

It gives you a view that is somewhat like the Slides Dockable taskbar. You see the slides you're working on and can move them around the presentation.

To go into the view click on Slide Sorter in the view tabs.

The Slides Dockable window will disappear, and you'll get previews of each slide:

You'll also see the Slide Sorter taskbar

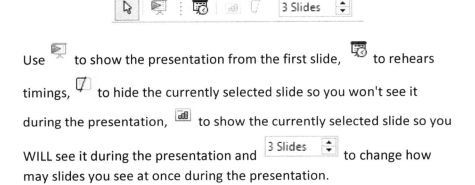

Use to show the presentation from the first slide, to rehears timings, to hide the currently selected slide so you won't see it during the presentation, to show the currently selected slide so you WILL see it during the presentation and 3 Slides to change how may slides you see at once during the presentation.

Moving slides

Click on a slide you want to move, press ctrl+x to cut it. Click onto the slide just before the point that you want to move it to (i.e. the slide that will precede the copied slide) and press Ctrl+v unless it's the last slide in which case click the mouse to the right of the last slide.

Alternatively, click on the slide you want to move and hold the mouse button dragging the mouse between the slides where you want it. Let go when you're happy.

How to use the Slide Navigator

I don't often use the Slide Navigator, but you can click on

Navigator Ctrl+Shift+F5 in the view menu to start it up. You'll see the Navigator dialogue

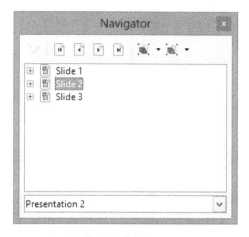

The navigation buttons  allow you to go to the first slide, back a slide, to the next slide and last slide in that order.

Clicking on ⊞ by a slide allows you to see the objects in that slide.

     ⊟ 🗒 Slide 1
         🔲 Shape 1
         🔲 Shape 2

Next Chapter

This chapter has provided information on different views that are supported by LibreOffice, and how to export files and print them.

In the next chapter I'm going to discuss some ways of standardising the design of your presentation using templates, master pages, and also a few other hints that may be useful when designing.

9 DESIGN CONSISTENCY

In this chapter I'm going to give you some tips on how to maintain consistency across a range of presentations, as well as how to use version control to prevent loss of data on corporate presentations:

- How to use a Master pages
- How to Create a Master Page
- How to create a Template
- How to use a Template
- How to edit a Template
- How to use the Presentation Wizard
- How to control versions

Many of these features aren't strictly 'necessary' because you can produce perfectly fine presentations without them but they do save time and can often result in a more professional look and feel for your document.

How to use an existing Master pages for a slide

Make sure you're in Normal view (if necessary by clicking Normal in the view tab).

In the Properties Dockable Window on the bottom right of the screen click Master Pages

You'll see the Master Pages Dockable Window

This is separated into Used in This Presentation (the master pages used in the presentation), recently used, and available for use.

Scroll down until you see a master page that looks good. You'll see the slide change so it uses the design elements of the new master page.

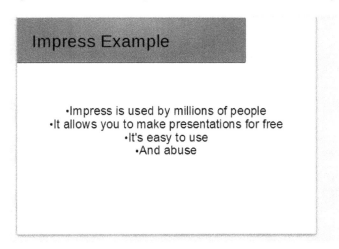

This feature is very useful since there are quite a few existing master pages that look very good. It's a simple way of improving the look of your presentation.

How to Create a Master Page

Hover your mouse over Master, and click on Slide Master.

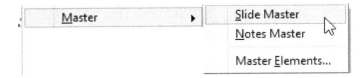

This will open up the Master View.

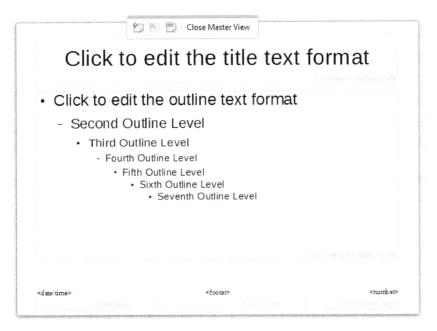

I find it easiest to choose a master page for the slide first which contains the right number / types of outline boxes. In the above example I'm just using a simple master page with a title and single placeholder text box.

In the Slides Dockable window right click on one of the slides and then click on New Master.

You'll see the new slide master appear in the slides Dockable window.

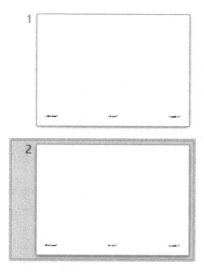

Right click on the new slide and click on 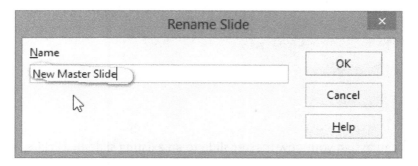 Rename Master. Type in the name.

Press OK. When you chose to change a slide to your new slide master this will come in handy.

If you highlight a line of text in one of the outline boxes:

- Click to edit the outline text format

And then change the font for that line of text Liberation Sans 32 or the font size, or any other attribute of the font then that will change the appearance of that type of text in any slides made from the master page.

You can move and resize a placeholder text box in the normal way - by clicking the outline and then moving the green squares (to resize) or holding the mouse button down and moving the box.

It's also easy to draw on the slide master - and any shapes you draw will appear on the slide. Similarly, you can insert an image like a logo or automatic fields such as date.

Designing a master slide isn't difficult. You use the same skills I've already taught you so far in the book.

Once you've finished creating your master slide, click on Close Master View in the Master View Dockable window:

You can assign your new master slide to an existing slide by clicking on the master slide icon in the properties window.

Delete a master page

You can only delete a master slide if it's not used in the slideshow. You need to be in Master View to change the Slide Master. Hover your mouse over Master, and click on Slide Master.

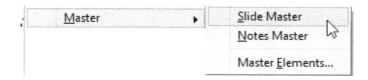

In the slides Dockable window, right click on the Master Slide you want to delete.

Click on ![Delete Master] to delete it. If it's used anywhere in the Slideshow you'll not be able to delete it until you change that slide's master page to another master page.

How to create a Template.

A template is in many ways like a normal presentation. You can edit it, add images and change the formatting, add master pages (in fact, that's recommended) and standard slides with company information or standard slides.

To create a template first create a new LibreOffice Impress presentation. Then edit the template until you're happy with it.

TIPS: When creating a template you're creating a document that you'll reuse. Instead of text you'll often have placeholder text that you'll adjust later on. Try to work out what is standard in the presentations you make then include only that 'standard' information.

For example, in this slide I've:

- Edited the master page fonts and background
- Included an image and,
- Included some placeholder text.

It's important to take your time making a template that reflects a standard design. This is especially the case when you're making one for a company where you will want to make a design that reflects marketing and corporate image.

Once you're happy with the design, hover your mouse over Templates in the File menu and click Save As Template

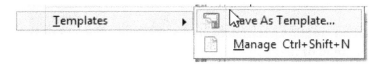

You'll see the Template Manager dialogue. Click on 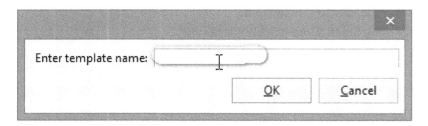 Save and LibreOffice will display a template name dialogue. Type in the name you want, then press enter.

You'll see the new template appear in the Template Manager. Click on

the cross [×] to close the window.

How to use a Template

Hover your mouse over new in the File menu then click on

.

Click on 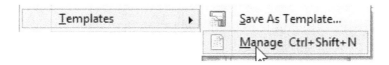 Presentations in the template type tab at the top of the Template Manager dialogue.

Double click on the template that you want to use (you may have to scroll down to find it if you have a lot of templates installed).

LibreOffice will open the template - alter any placeholder text and edit the new presentation as normal. It's as simple as that. Once you've finished save the new presentation.

Hint: Once you create a file from a template, any changes to the template don't affect the file. So be careful if you edit templates - old presentations may not be up to date!

How to edit a Template

Hover your mouse over Templates in the File menu, and then click on Manage.

Templates	▶	🗒	Save As Template...
		📄	Manage Ctrl+Shift+N

Click on the Presentations tab in the Template Type tab if necessary to display your current template.

Find the template you want to edit, scrolling down if necessary, and be careful to single click on it (double clicking will open up a new instance of the template).

At the top of the template manager dialogue you'll see a taskbar:

To delete the template, click on a confirmation dialogue will be displayed

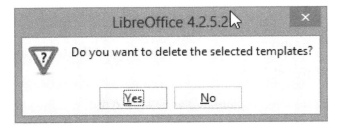

Click on yes if you are sure; remember this is a permanent decision. You can't easy undelete a template if you delete it.

To edit the template click .

Your template will open. Remember to save it once you've finished editing it.

How to use the Presentation Wizard

Hover your mouse over Wizards in the File menu, then click on 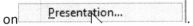 .

You'll see the presentation Wizard appear:

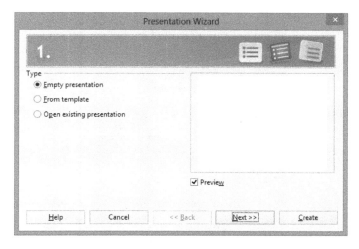

There are three options: Empty Presentation (where you're starting a presentation from scratch), From Template (where you're using a template) or open existing presentation.

It's my feeling that because the template manager overrides design decisions made during template creation it's often best to simply make a new presentation from the template (using the steps I've shown above). I therefore only use the Presentation Wizard while making an Empty Presentation.

But you can use either of the other two options.

Step 1

If you leave the Wizard with ⊙ Empty presentation toggled on, you'll start making a presentation from scratch.

Clicking the circle next to ○ From template to toggle it on will show a list of templates. Click on the one that you want.

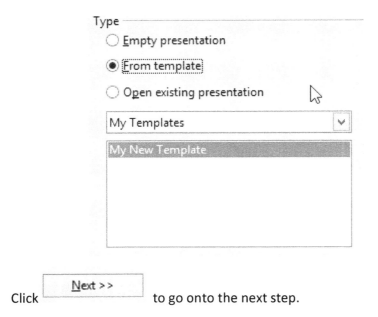

Click [Next >>] to go onto the next step.

Step 2

If you want to change the background, select an appropriate one from the Slide Design list. A preview on the right will show you what your decision looks like. Changing the background will override any decision you made during your template design.

The next option is the output medium. If you're going to display on a screen select that, otherwise select the option that you need by clicking on the circle to the left of the option.

Select an output medium

⦿ Original   ○ Screen

○ Overhead sheet   ○ Slide

○ Paper   ○ Widescreen

Check the Preview window, then click [Next >>] .

Step 3

Click on the down arrow next to effect

Effect 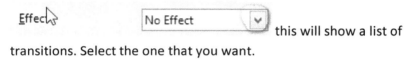 this will show a list of transitions. Select the one that you want.

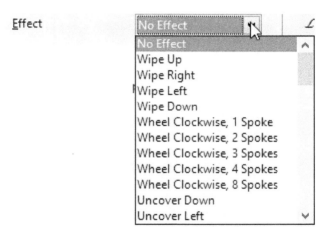

Then click on the down arrow next to speed

Speed  to chose from slow, medium or fast transition. You can see the effect of your decision in the preview window to the right of the dialogue.

I suggest leaving the Select the presentation type as default and then rehearsing timings before you decide how long each slide should last if you choose to do automatic transitions.

Click 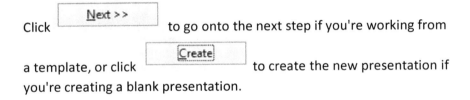 to go onto the next step if you're working from a template, or click to create the new presentation if you're creating a blank presentation.

Step 4.

This step is self explanatory. Type in the name of your company, the subject, and any ideas you want to explore.

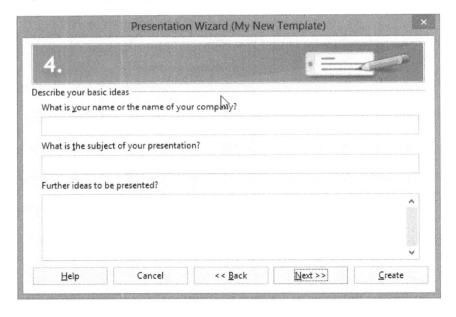

Note that if you enter information in here it will override the information in your template. You may simply chose to ignore this step and leave the information in the template as it is.

Click  to go onto the next step.

Step 5.

In this step you can untick (by clicking in the box) any slide from the template that you don't want to include in your presentation.

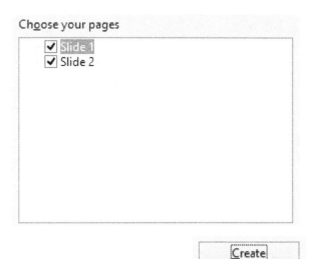

Once you're happy with your choices, click [Create] .

You can edit the template you've created using the Presentation Wizard in the normal way.

How to control versions

LibreOffice Impress provides you with a facility to prevent yourself losing work when you're editing a presentation. You can save versions that can then be rolled back. Start the Version dialogue by clicking  in the file menu.

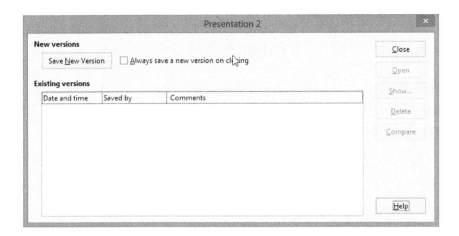

Creating a new version

You can set LibreOffice Impress to automatically generate a version every time you close the program by clicking on the highlighted

square  to toggle on automatic saving.

Otherwise, clicking ___Save New Version___ will manually save a new version.

You can write comments in the highlighted box

The version will show up in the existing version list

Existing versions

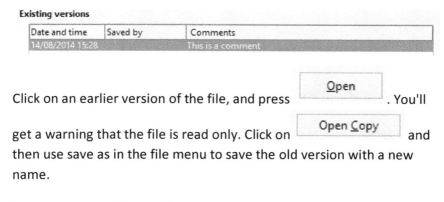

Date and time	Saved by	Comments
14/08/2014 15:28		This is a comment

Click on an earlier version of the file, and press Open . You'll

get a warning that the file is read only. Click on Open Copy and

then use save as in the file menu to save the old version with a new

name.

You've recovered the version.

You can delete a version by clicking on it in the list and then clicking

 .

So Long, and thanks!

Well, that's it.

In this book I hope that you've learned the basics of using LibreOffice
Impress. You should be able to create professional presentations and
have a bit of fun at the same time. While I haven't covered everything
that LibreOffice has to offer I hope that I've covered everything you
need to start using it.

I really enjoyed writing this book, and I hope that you enjoy using
LibreOffice Impress! If you've got any questions or comments feel free
to email me at thomasecclestone@yahoo.co.uk .

ABOUT THE AUTHOR

Thomas Ecclestone is a software programmer and technical writer from Kent in the south east of England. In his spare time he looks after a herd of Hebridean sheep and lives on a smallholding where he writes book and looks after a wildflower meadow.

You can find out more about his current projects at thomasecclestone.co.uk

www.ingramcontent.com/pod-product-compliance
Lightning Source LLC
Chambersburg PA
CBHW071000050326
40689CB00014B/3435